A Resource Guide on Racial Profiling Data Collection Systems

Promising Practices and Lessons Learned

Deborah Ramirez
Jack McDevitt
Amy Farrell
Northeastern University

November 2000   Monograph   NCJ 184768

Foreword

For the past 8 years, we have seen a steady decline in the crime rate in nearly every community in America. Even with the advances in crime prevention and law enforcement, however, there are instances in which distrust and tensions between the police and the community are high, and these tensions affect all aspects of the criminal justice system. One of the major causes of this mistrust is the controversial practice of racial profiling.

The guarantee to all persons of equal protection under the law is one of the most fundamental principles of our democratic society. Law enforcement officers should not endorse or act upon stereotypes, attitudes, or beliefs that a person's race, ethnicity, or national origin increases that person's general propensity to act unlawfully. There is no tradeoff between effective law enforcement and protection of the civil rights of all Americans; we can and must have both.

One of the ways that law enforcement agencies are addressing concerns and allegations regarding discriminatory policing is through data collection. By collecting information on the nature, character, and demographics of police enforcement practices, we enhance our ability to assess the appropriate application of the authority and broad discretion entrusted to law enforcement.

In June 1999, when President Clinton and U.S. Attorney General Reno convened the conference *Strengthening Police-Community Relationships*, only a few jurisdictions—including San Diego, San Jose, and the state of North Carolina—had voluntarily agreed to collect traffic-stop data. When a followup meeting on racial profiling and data collection was held this past February, more than 100 jurisdictions indicated that they had plans to collect data on traffic or pedestrian stops.

To encourage voluntary data collection, the U.S. Department of Justice set about developing a resource guide on this subject. The result is this publication, *A Resource Guide on Racial Profiling Data Collection Systems*, prepared by staff of Northeastern University. This document provides an overview of the nature of racial profiling; a description of data collection and its purpose; current activities in California, New Jersey, North Carolina, and Great Britain; and recommendations for the future.

Our hope is that this resource guide will assist jurisdictions in developing and implementing their own data collection systems. Our ultimate goals are to restore trust in the police and to ensure that all citizens are treated equally by law enforcement officers.

Nancy E. Gist
Director
Bureau of Justice Assistance
U.S. Department of Justice

Acknowledgments

Deborah Ramirez, Jack McDevitt, and Amy Farrell would like to acknowledge the assistance of many individuals and agencies. In particular, we thank Attorney General Janet Reno and the U.S. Department of Justice for supporting research on racial profiling data collection efforts. We appreciate the support of Richard Jerome, Deputy Associate Attorney General, and Karen Stevens, Counsel to the Assistant Attorney General, who facilitated development of this project; the Bureau of Justice Assistance for providing the resources for this research; and Northeastern University for enabling our involvement with this project. Most of all we are grateful to the members of those law enforcement and state agencies who generously shared their time and knowledge with us.

Contents

Introduction

On June 9–10, 1999, President Bill Clinton, Attorney General Janet Reno, civil rights leaders, police, and other government leaders participated in the *Strengthening Police-Community Relationships* conference in Washington, D.C. During the conference, President Clinton called racial profiling a "morally indefensible, deeply corrosive practice" and further stated that "racial profiling is in fact the opposite of good police work, where actions are based on hard facts, not stereotypes. It is wrong, it is destructive, and it must stop."[1] As a result of increased national concern over racial profiling, the President directed federal agencies to begin gathering data on the race and ethnicity of persons stopped for future analysis.

At a later session of the same conference, participants discussed the design and implementation of racial profiling data collection systems. That discussion featured presentations by state and local jurisdictions where efforts were already under way to collect data on the race, ethnicity, and gender of the individuals police stop. This guide is an outgrowth of that breakout session. As its title suggests, the guide is designed to provide law enforcement, state and local elected officials, civil rights leaders, community organizations, and other local stakeholders with strategies and practices for gathering and analyzing data about police stops. By providing information about the nature, characteristics, and demographics of police enforcement patterns, these data collection efforts have the potential for shifting the rhetoric surrounding racial profiling from accusations, anecdotal stories, and stereotypes to a more rational discussion about the appropriate allocation of police resources. Well-planned and comprehensive data collection efforts can serve as a catalyst for nurturing and shaping this type of community and police discussion.

This guide is a blueprint that police and communities can use to develop data collection systems. It offers practical information about implementing these systems and analyzing the data. The guide is not intended to serve as a comprehensive and thorough inventory of all existing data collection systems. It focuses on providing detailed descriptions of data collection efforts in a few selected sites: San Jose, California, which has designed a simple letter-code system allowing information to be collected verbally (via radio) or by computer; San Diego, California, which utilizes an online data collection system; North Carolina, the first state to collect data on traffic stops pursuant to state legislation; Great Britain, which uses a paper-based system to collect information on both traffic and pedestrian stops and searches; and New Jersey, which is collecting information on traffic-stops pursuant to a consent decree with the U.S. Department of Justice (DOJ). These sites were first identified by DOJ in preparation for the conference and represent various population sizes and geographic locations.

Site visits were later made to obtain further information about each site's data collection process.

Since the conference, there has been a flurry of activity in this area and hundreds of jurisdictions have begun to initiate data collection efforts. For example, Connecticut, Kansas, Missouri, and Washington have passed state legislation requiring state police and/or local police agencies to record and make public the racial and ethnic pattern of their traffic-stops. In California, approximately 75 agencies, including the California Highway Patrol, have begun to implement data collection systems. Florida Governor Jeb Bush directed the Florida Highway Patrol to begin collecting traffic-stop data in 2000. In August 1999, Houston's police department began to collect data on its traffic and pedestrian stops. Moreover, several other cities and towns have voluntarily agreed to implement data collection systems, including San Francisco, California; Tallahassee, Florida; Dearborn, Michigan; and Richmond, Virginia. In addition, some states have begun to implement statewide systems, including Michigan and Washington. Pursuant to federal consent decrees and settlements, Montgomery County, Maryland; Steubenville, Ohio; and Pittsburgh, Pennsylvania, have also implemented data collection systems. As part of settlements with the American Civil Liberties Union (ACLU), the Maryland State Police (MSP) and the Philadelphia Police Department have also begun to collect data.

This resource guide is organized into four main sections:

❑ Chapter 2: An introduction to the nature of the problem of racial profiling.

❑ Chapter 3: A general description of data collection and its limitations.

❑ Chapter 4: Study-site descriptions and analysis.

❑ Chapter 5: Recommendations and future goals.

The "selected site" approach of this resource guide is intended to encourage and guide police and communities as they begin to take action to evaluate allegations of racial profiling and to help police and communities learn from one another's experiences and successes. To facilitate this exchange of ideas, contact information is provided for each site described in this guide. To promote the continued exchange of facts, forms, and new data collection systems, one recommendation of this guide is to create a Web site for sharing information about racial profiling and data collection.

The Nature of the Problem of Racial Profiling

The problem of racial profiling is complex and multifaceted. Dedicated police officers and professional police practices have contributed to making our communities safer. The majority of police officers are hard-working public servants who perform a dangerous job with dedication and honor; however, the perception that some police officers are engaging in racial profiling has created resentment and distrust of the police, particularly in communities of color. These communities applaud the benefits of community policing in reducing crime, but they also believe that truly effective policing will only be achieved when police both protect their neighborhoods from crime and respect the civil liberties of all residents. When law enforcement practices are perceived to be biased, unfair, or disrespectful, communities of color are less willing to trust and confide in police officers, report crimes, participate in problem-solving activities, be witnesses at trials, or serve on juries.

Defining Racial Profiling

When seeking to determine whether allegations of racial profiling are accurate, any analysis concerning the nature and scope of the problem depends on the definition of racial profiling used. For this guide, racial profiling is defined as any police-initiated action that relies on the race, ethnicity, or national origin rather than the behavior of an individual or information that leads the police to a particular individual who has been identified as being, or having been, engaged in criminal activity.

There is almost uniform consensus on two corollary principles that follow from adopting this definition of racial profiling: police may not use racial or ethnic stereotypes as factors in selecting whom to stop-and-search, and police may use race or ethnicity to determine whether a person matches a specific description of a particular suspect.[2]

Developing consensus on whether race can be used when police are addressing a crime committed by a group of individuals who share racial or ethnic characteristics is more difficult. Of course, when police know that a particular individual is a member of a criminal organization, police may legitimately use that information as a factor in the totality of the circumstances that may indicate ongoing criminal activity. For example, many criminal organizations are composed of persons with similar ethnic, racial, or national origin characteristics. Under the definition used in this guide, however, if police use a person's race, ethnicity, or national origin in determining whether a specific individual is a member of a criminal organization, they have engaged in racial profiling.

Nature and Extent of Perceptions of Racial Profiling

In the late 1990s, the American news media exploded with coverage of the problem of racial profiling. Indeed, the allegations have become so common that the community of color has labeled the phenomenon with the derisive term "driving while black" or "driving while brown." Front-page news stories and editorials in both the national and local press began to illustrate the individual and social costs of racial profiling.

National surveys have confirmed that most Americans, regardless of race, believe that racial profiling is a significant social problem. According to a Gallup Poll released on December 9, 1999, more than half of Americans polled believed that police actively engage in the practice of racial profiling and, more significantly, 81 percent of them said they disapprove of the practice.[3] In a national sample of adults, 59 percent said that racial profiling is widespread.[4] When the responses to the survey question were broken down by race, 56 percent of Whites and 77 percent of Blacks responded that racial profiling was pervasive. Additionally, the Gallup survey asked respondents how often they perceived having been stopped by the police based on their race alone. Six percent of Whites and 42 percent of Blacks responded that they had been stopped by the police because of their race, and 72 percent of Black men between ages 18 and 34 believed they had been stopped because of their race.

Recent survey data also confirm a strong connection between perceptions of race-based stops by police and animosity toward local and state law enforcement. In addition to gathering data on individual perceptions of stops by the police, the 1999 Gallup Poll asked respondents how favorably they viewed the police. Eighty-five percent of White respondents had a favorable response toward local police and 87 percent of White respondents had a favorable response to state police. Black respondents, overall, had a less favorable opinion of both state and local police, with just 58 percent having a favorable opinion of the local police and 64 percent having a favorable response to the state police. Fifty-three percent of Black men between ages 18 and 34 said they had been treated unfairly by local police.

Similarly, a 12-city survey conducted by DOJ in 1998 demonstrated that, although most people in the African American community felt satisfied with police services in their neighborhoods, their level of dissatisfaction was approximately twice that of the White community.[5] This wide schism in all 12 cities surveyed indicates the need for law enforcement to work harder to restore the confidence of communities of color in the critical work being done by law enforcement. Police departments that fail to address the perception of racially discriminatory policing within minority neighborhoods may find their law enforcement efforts undermined.

Evidence of Racial Profiling

Anecdotal and empirical evidence confirm national perceptions about the pervasiveness of racial profiling. To better understand the issues associated with identifying racial profiling in police stops, concerns about police discretion have been broken into two stages: an officer's decision to stop a vehicle or person and the actions of the officer during the stop. The second issue may include a number of questions: Are passengers and drivers ordered to step out of the car? Is the suspect treated with respect? Are police questioning the occupants about subjects unrelated to the traffic-stop violation? Were drug-sniffing dogs summoned to the scene? Did the officer request permission to search the car and its contents? How long did the encounter last? The answers to these and other questions are critical for understanding the complexities and nuances of racial profiling. Evidence from anecdotal accounts and statistical studies has begun to address these important issues.

Anecdotal Evidence

Personal anecdotes and stories help illustrate the experiences of those who believe they have been stopped because of racial profiling and, in turn, give rise to a set of common concerns about police stop-and-search practices. A 1999 report by David Harris, *Driving While Black: Racial Profiling on Our Nation's Highways*, cites numerous accounts of disparate treatment toward minorities by police from a variety of state and local jurisdictions.[6] A sample of these accounts illustrates the emotional impact of such incidents.

The concern that police stop drivers because they or their passengers do not appear to "match" the type of vehicle they occupy is common in racial profiling accounts. This "driving in the wrong car" concern is illustrated by the experiences of Dr. Elmo Randolph, a 42-year-old African-American dentist, who commutes from Bergen County to his office near Newark, New Jersey. Since 1991, he has been stopped by New Jersey troopers more than 50 times. Randolph does not drive at excessive speeds and claims he has never been issued a ticket.[7] Instead, troopers approach his gold BMW, request his license and registration, and ask him if he has any drugs or weapons in his car. The experience of Randolph and many other minority drivers on New Jersey's highways led to the recent consent decree and settlement between the state of New Jersey and DOJ. As a result of the settlement, New Jersey State Police (NJSP) are collecting data on the race and ethnicity of persons stopped by state troopers and improving their supervision and training.

Another common complaint is that police stop people of color traveling through predominately White areas because the police believe that people of color do not "belong" in certain neighborhoods and may be engaged in criminal activity. This type of profiling was reported by Alvin Penn, the

African-American deputy president of the Connecticut State Senate. In 1996, a Trumbull, Connecticut, police officer stopped Penn as he drove his van through this predominately White suburban town. After reviewing Penn's license and registration, the officer asked Penn if he knew which town he was in (Bridgeport, the state's largest city, where Blacks and Latinos comprise 75 percent of the population, borders Trumbull, which is 98 percent White). Penn, recalling that he had been turning around on a dead-end street when the officer stopped him, responded by asking why he needed to know which town he was in. The officer told him that he was not required to give Penn a reason for the stop and that, if he made an issue of it, the officer would cite him for speeding.[8] Three years after this incident, Penn sponsored legislation that made Connecticut the second state to begin collecting data on the demographics of individuals stopped by state police.

By far the most common complaint by members of communities of color is that they are being stopped for petty traffic violations such as underinflated tires, failure to signal properly before switching lanes, vehicle equipment failures, speeding less than 10 miles above the speed limit, or having an illegible license plate. One example of this is the account of Robert Wilkins, a Harvard Law School graduate and a public defender in Washington, D.C., who went to a family funeral in Ohio in May 1992. On the return trip, he and his aunt, uncle, and 29-year-old cousin rented a Cadillac for the trip home. His cousin was stopped for speeding in western Maryland while driving 60 miles per hour in a 55-mile-per-hour zone of the interstate. The group was forced to stand on the side of the interstate in the rain for an extended period while officers and drug-sniffing dogs searched their car. Nothing was found. Wilkins, represented by the ACLU, filed suit and received a settlement from the state of Maryland.[9]

Although this small sample of anecdotal evidence does not prove that police officers actively engage in racial profiling, it is representative of the thousands of personal stories cataloged in newspaper articles, interviews, ACLU commentary, and court battles.

Empirical Research on Racial Profiling

In addition to a growing body of individual accounts of racial profiling, scholars have begun examining the relationship between police stop-and-search practices and racial characteristics of individual drivers. The majority of empirical research collected to date has been used in expert testimony accompanying lawsuits. *Wilkins* v. *Maryland State Police* (1993) was one of the first cases to introduce empirical evidence of racial profiling into the court record.

In 1995 and 1996, as a result of Wilkins' settlement with the Maryland State Police (MSP), Dr. John Lamberth, a professor of psychology at Temple University, conducted an analysis of police searches along I–95 in Maryland.

Using data released by MSP pursuant to the settlement, Lamberth compared the population of people searched and arrested with those violating traffic laws on Maryland highways. He constructed a violator sample using both stationary and rolling surveys of drivers violating the legal speed limit on a selected portion of the interstate. His violator survey indicated that 74.7 percent of speeders were White, while 17.5 percent were Black.[10] In contrast, according to MSP data, Blacks constituted 79.2 percent of the drivers searched. Lamberth concluded that the data revealed "dramatic and highly statistically significant disparities between the percentage of Black I–95 motorists legitimately subject to stop by the Maryland State Police and the percentage of Black motorists detained and searched by troopers on this roadway."[11]

Empirical data on stop-and-search practices in New Jersey also originated through actions of the court. In the late 1980s and early 1990s, Black drivers were reporting that they were being stopped disproportionately by New Jersey troopers. In response to these complaints, in 1994, the Gloucester County public defender's office, while representing Pedro Soto and others, filed a motion to suppress evidence obtained in a series of searches, alleging that the searches were unlawful because they were part of a pattern and practice of racial profiling by New Jersey troopers.[12] As part of that litigation, the defendants received traffic-stop and arrest data compiled by NJSP in selected locations from 1988 through 1991.[13] Lamberth served as the statistical expert for the defendants and conducted a comparative violator survey to weigh the percentage of Blacks stopped and arrested by New Jersey troopers against a comparative percentage of Blacks who violated traffic laws on New Jersey highways. His analyses found that Blacks comprised 13.5 percent of the New Jersey Turnpike population and 15 percent of the drivers speeding. In contrast, Blacks represented 35 percent of those stopped and 73.2 percent of those arrested. In other words, in New Jersey, Black drivers were disproportionally more likely to be stopped and arrested than White drivers. The Superior Court of New Jersey relied on Lamberth's study in its decision to suppress the evidence seized by New Jersey troopers in 19 consolidated criminal prosecutions and concurred with his opinion that the troopers relied on race in stopping and searching turnpike motorists.

Recent data collection efforts in New Jersey and New York have confirmed the independent empirical findings used in court cases. In April 1999, the Attorney General of New Jersey issued a report indicating that New Jersey troopers had engaged in racial profiling along the New Jersey Turnpike.[14] This report tracked the racial breakdowns of traffic-stops between 1997 and 1998. The information indicated that people of color constituted 40.6 percent of the stops made on the turnpike. Although few stops resulted in a search, 77.2 percent of those individuals searched were people of color. An analysis of the productivity of these searches indicated that 10.5 percent of the searches that involved White motorists resulted in an arrest or seizure and that 13.5 percent of the searches involving Black motorists resulted in arrest or seizure. Finally, the New Jersey report demonstrated that minority motorists were more likely to be involved in consent searches than nonminority motorists. Eighty percent of consent searches involved minority motorists.[15]

In December 1999, New York Attorney General Eliot Spitzer released the results of an investigation by his office of the "stop and frisk" practices in New York City. It showed that Blacks and Latinos were much more likely to be stopped and searched even when the statistics were adjusted to reflect differing criminal participation rates in some neighborhoods.[16] After reviewing 175,000 incidents in which citizens were stopped by the police during the 15-month period that ended in March 1999, the attorney general found that Blacks were stopped six times more often than Whites, while Latinos were stopped four times more often. Blacks made up 25 percent of the city population but 50 percent of the people stopped and 67 percent of the people stopped by the New York City Street Crimes Unit.[17]

International data suggest that racial profiling is not an isolated American experience. A 1998 study by the British Government's Home Office examined the racial and ethnic demographics of the stop-and-search patterns of 43 police forces in England and Wales. The study indicated that Blacks were 7.5 times more likely to be stopped and searched and 4 times more likely to be arrested than Whites.[18] This is true even though, according to census population figures, Great Britain is 93 percent White and 7 percent ethnic minority.[19] Although the high proportion of searches of people of color has been a constant feature of police searches in London, England, and elsewhere, the proportion of searches that result in an arrest does not differ by race or ethnicity. That is, the arrest rate differs little regardless of whether the search was of a White or Black person. In London, the arrest rate was 11.1 percent for light-skinned Europeans, 11.4 percent for dark-skinned Europeans, and 11.7 percent for Black people. In the case of Asians, the arrest rate was lowest at 9.4 percent.[20]

Anecdotal and empirical evidence has helped state and local activists, community members, and government officials understand the problem of racial profiling and has raised new questions about police stop-and-search practices. However, more expansive and systematic data collection is needed to address the concerns surrounding police practices of racial profiling.

Origin of Racial Profiling and the Complexities of Police Discretion

Although empirical research, anecdotal evidence, and survey data confirm the existence of racial profiling as a social problem, many still question how such profiling could arise. Throughout all areas of their daily routine, police exercise a great deal of individual discretion. Within the area of traffic-stops, for example, police must use reasoned judgment in deciding which cars to stop from among the universe of cars being operated in violation of the law. Since many traffic enforcement and vehicle code laws apply to all cars on the road, and since more vehicles are being operated in violation of the local traffic laws than police have the resources to stop them, officers have a wide discretion in selecting which cars to stop.

Many traffic officers say that by following any vehicle for 1 or 2 minutes, they can observe a basis on which to stop it.[21] Many police departments have not developed formal, written, standards directing officers on how to use this discretion. Instead, officers often develop ad hoc methods of winnowing suspicious from innocent motorists. This intuition, often learned by young officers observing the actions of more experienced officers, can vary widely across individual officers even within a particular department. Police departments often use traffic-stops as a means of ferreting out illicit drugs and weapons. Consequently, some officers routinely use traffic stops as a means of tracking down drug or gun couriers. These discretionary decisions are seldom documented and rarely reviewed. As a result, individual officers are infrequently made accountable for these decisions.

Levels of Police Discretion

Several factors may influence an officer's decision to stop-and-search an individual, but the various types of potential scenarios can easily be broken down into high- and low-discretion realms. Traffic and pedestrian stops can be viewed on a continuum from low-discretion stops, in which an officer's decision not to make a stop is limited, to high-discretion stops, in which the decision to stop someone is often based on an officer's experiences in the field.

Low discretion. Although the nature and scope of low-discretion stops vary by place and context, they are common in policing. Low-discretion stops can include those based on externally generated reports of a crime or suspicious activity, such as when a victim describes a particular suspect. In the traffic-stop context, for jurisdictions in which traffic enforcement is a priority, speeding more than 10 miles above the speed limit or running a red light may also be placed in the category of low-discretion stops. Some jurisdictions have actually calculated the percentage of stops that fall in this low-discretion category. The New York attorney general's *Stop and Frisk* study, for example, shows that only 30 percent of the stops were based on victims' descriptions.[22] Similarly, in London, England, only 25 percent of searches in selected study sites were considered low discretion.[23]

High discretion. The complexities of police discretion emerge more often in the high-discretion stop category. In the traffic-stop context, these stops include checks for underinflated tires, safety belt warnings, failures to signal lane changes, and other minor vehicle code and nonmoving violations. In the pedestrian-stop context, high-discretion stops involve those who may look suspicious but are not engaged in any specific criminal violation or activities. These high-discretion stops invite both intentional and unintentional abuses. Police are just as subject to the racial and ethnic stereotypes they learn from our culture as any other citizen. Unless documented, such stops create an environment that allows the use of stereotypes to go undetected.

The Perception That Minorities Are More Likely To Carry Contraband

The perception that African Americans, Hispanics, Asians, and other minorities are more likely to carry drugs than their White counterparts intensifies the complexities of police discretion in stops and searches.[24] The escalating pressure from the war on drugs has led some police officers to target people of color whom police believe to be disproportionally involved in drug use and trafficking. Although some members of the police community suggest that race-based searches are justified because more minority drivers are found with contraband, the empirical evidence amassed to date tends to discredit such arguments.[25] In Lamberth's study on I–95 in Maryland, he found that 28.4 percent of Black drivers and passengers who were searched were found with contraband and 28.8 percent of White drivers and passengers who were searched were found with contraband.[26] Thus, the probability of finding contraband was the same for Blacks and Whites. Race did not matter. According to the New Jersey attorney general's *Interim Report* (April 1999), the "hit rates" at which contraband was found among those searched did not differ significantly by race. Only 10.5 percent of the searches of Whites resulted in an arrest or seizure compared to a rate of 13.5 percent for Black motorists.[27] Similarly, in the New York study of "stop and frisk" practices, between 1998 and 1999, the attorney general found that 12.6 percent of Whites stopped were arrested, compared to only 10.5 percent of Blacks and 11.3 percent of Latinos.[28] In a recent U.S. Customs Service study, nationwide data revealed that, while 43 percent of those searched were either Black or Latino, the hit rates for Blacks and Latinos were actually lower than the hit rates for Whites. The study found that 6.7 percent of Whites, 6.3 percent of Blacks, and 2.8 percent of Hispanics had contraband. This finding is particularly surprising because the study does not involve car stops, but involves stops and searches in airports. Presumably, if the perception that drug couriers are more likely to be Black or Latino were true, a widespread survey of airport searches should reveal differing hit rates.[29] Similarly, in London, England, the probability of finding contraband as a result of a search did not significantly differ among races.[30] Although sound empirical research on the relationship between race and hit rates for contraband is limited, to date the evidence indicates that Blacks and Latinos are no more likely than Whites to be in possession of narcotics or other contraband.[31]

In many cases, disproportionate minority arrests for drug possession and distribution have fueled perceptions by police and others that race is an appropriate factor in the decision to stop or search an individual.[32] However, existing data on the productivity of searches across racial groups suggest that stop-and-search practices have become a game of "search and you will find." Police officers who aggressively and disproportionately search people of color will arrest more people of color than Whites, not because of differences in behavior, but because they are stopping and searching many more people of color than Whites. Regardless of whether the perception that Blacks and Latinos are more likely to be found in possession of contraband could be empirically verified, United States laws do not, and should not, permit race to be used as a basis for stopping and searching individuals.[33]

General Description of Data Collection Goals and Limitations

In response to allegations of racial profiling, some communities have begun to track the race, ethnicity, and gender of those who are stopped and/or searched by police officers. This chapter examines the feasibility of having law enforcement collect data to determine whether racial profiling exists in a particular setting.

Data Collection Systems

Why would a law enforcement entity begin to collect data about the demographics of its stops? Reasons vary. The most obvious one is that in the long run the systematic collection of statistics and information regarding law enforcement activities support community policing by building trust and respect for the police in the community. The only way to move the discussion about racial profiling from rhetoric and accusation to a more rational dialogue about appropriate enforcement strategies is to collect the information that will either allay community concerns about the activities of the police or help communities ascertain the scope and magnitude of the problem. When police begin to collect information about the racial and ethnic demographics of their stops, they demonstrate that they have nothing to hide and retain their credibility. Once data are collected, they become catalysts for an informed community-police discussion about the appropriate allocation of police resources. Such a process promises to promote neighborhood policing.

Implementing a data collection system also sends a clear message to the entire police community, as well as to the larger community, that racial profiling is inconsistent with effective policing and equal protection. When implemented properly, this system helps to shape and develop a training program to educate officers about the conscious and subconscious use of racial and ethnic stereotypes and to promote courteous and respectful police-citizen encounters.

When implemented as part of a comprehensive early warning system, data collection processes can identify potential police misconduct and deter it. By detecting and addressing instances of disparate treatment of persons of color by the police, law enforcement organizations may be able to prevent the development of a systemic pattern and practice of discrimination.

Finally, a data collection system can also improve police productivity by enabling police to assess and study the most effective stop-and-search practices. It can provide police with information about the types of stops being made by officers, the proportion of police time spent on high-discretion stops, and the results of such steps. It may identify certain strategies to improve the likelihood that a stop will result in an arrest or seizure of contraband. It will also enable police and the community to assess the quantity and quality of police-citizen encounters.

Although no written policy can anticipate all situations and mechanistic adherence to formal procedures could chill the use of sound judgment and experience, data collection could help officers understand practices that they may be undertaking subconsciously. Additionally, data collection can assist departments in developing strategic ways to use the power at their disposal.

Potential Challenges in Implementing a Data Collection System

There are myriad benefits from implementing a data collection system, but there are also some potential challenges. The most common have been articulated as follows:

❑ How can officers determine the race or ethnicity of the citizens they stop in the least confrontational manner and without increasing the intrusiveness of the stop?

❑ What budgetary, time, and paperwork burdens will data collection impose on police departments?

❑ Will data collection procedures result in police "disengagement" by leading police officers to scale down the number of legitimate stops and searches they conduct?

❑ How can departments ensure the accuracy of data collection procedures and be certain that reporting requirements are not circumvented by officers who fail to file required reports or who report erroneous information?

❑ How can departments collect enough information to provide a refined, contextualized analysis without unduly burdening line officers?

❑ How can departments ensure full compliance by line officers and deal effectively with any officer resistance?

❑ Will the data that are collected be used for research and training purposes only or will they be used to discipline officers and facilitate lawsuits?

❑ Will the data be analyzed and compared with an appropriate measure of the statistically correct representative population? How do you ascertain and define the parameters of that population?

Since several jurisdictions have already begun to collect data on the race, ethnicity, and gender of the persons police stop, the next section of this guide provides information about existing data collection systems and how jurisdictions have addressed and overcome these potential challenges.

Study Site Experiences and Analyses

The San Jose Experience

San Jose is the 3rd largest city in California and the 11th largest city in the nation. Nestled in California's Silicon Valley, it is a large, culturally diverse urban community with a population estimated at 900,000. San Jose's population is approximately 43 percent White, 31 percent Hispanic, 21 percent Asian, and 4.5 percent African American.[34] In 1999, the officers of San Jose's police force made approximately 100,000 traffic-stops.[35]

Precipitating Events

Like other cities, San Jose was faced with rising community complaints about racial profiling. The city's independent police auditor, Teresa Guerreo-Daley, was receiving about 500 complaints each year concerning alleged profile stops.[36] However, these complaints were rarely sustained because there was no evidence about the reason for the stops other than police statements. Although some complaints were probably unwarranted and others might have been retaliation against the police, no one could determine whether there was a problem.

Meanwhile, in 1999, State Senator Kevin Murray reintroduced a bill into the California Legislature requiring that all state law enforcement agencies collect data on the racial and ethnic demographics of their traffic-stops.[37] The bill required police to collect information and data surrounding vehicle stops, including information on searches, the results of searches, and information about passengers. Although the bill was ultimately vetoed, it was part of what galvanized San Jose Police Chief William Landsdowne to create a simpler data collection system. He felt that the proposed legislatively created system was too onerous and thought that the implementation of a simpler system might convince legislators to modify the proposed system.

Another impetus for San Jose to begin gathering data about the demographics of their stops was a highly publicized incident that occurred on March 9, 1999. On that date, Michael McBride, a Black youth minister, asserted that he was the victim of a racial profiling stop and a subsequent search and assault by San Jose police officers. An internal affairs investigation concluded that the department could neither prove nor disprove McBride's allegations.

In response to community complaints and the prospect of a legislatively imposed data collection system, on March 24, Chief Lansdowne announced that San Jose would become the second California city to embark voluntarily on tracking the race, gender, age, and reason for stopping motorists. Chief Lansdowne wanted to respond to the community's perception that people of color were being stopped because of their race and to demonstrate to the community that the San Jose police did not "do business that way."[38]

Data Collection Process

On June 1, 1999, San Jose began to implement a data collection system that focused on four key pieces of information: race/ethnicity of the driver, gender, age (adult or minor), and the reason for the stop. It is a simple system designed to minimize the burden on line officers.

Since 1996, every patrol car in the San Jose Police Department (SJPD) has been equipped with a mobile data terminal (MDT). San Jose's data collection system, however, can be used with or without the MDT units. Using a system based on letter codes, the traffic-stop data collection system is designed to collect and relay information verbally (via police radio) or by typing the information into the MDT in the patrol car. This system eliminates the need for officers to complete or collect written forms or reports.

Traffic-stop protocol before June 1999. Even before the data collection system was implemented, whenever officers made a traffic-stop, they advised the communications dispatcher via radio or MDT that a traffic-stop was being made. At that time, the officer would tell the dispatcher the driver's gender. After the stop was completed, the officer would use an alpha code to indicate to the dispatcher the result of the stop (e.g., whether a citation was issued, whether an arrest was made). For instance, the officer would clear a call by stating on the radio "10–98 D–David." The "10–98" meant that the call was being cleared, and the "D–David" meant that a traffic citation had been issued.

The new data collection system. Under the new data collection system, three additional alpha codes are being used by officers clearing a stop. These new alpha codes indicate the reason for the stop, the race of the driver, and whether the driver is an adult or a juvenile.[39] For example, under the new system an officer clears a call by stating "10–98 D–David, V–Victor, W–William, A–Adam." "D–David" means that a moving violation citation was issued; "V–Victor" means the reason for the stop was a vehicle code violation; "W–William" means the race of the individual driver was White; and "A–Adam" means the driver was an adult. This information can be relayed to the dispatcher via radio or the MDT unit.

SJPD uses the following codes to indicate race and ethnicity:

A = Asian American.

B = African American.

H = Hispanic.

I = Native American.

O = Other.

P = Pacific Islander.

S = Middle Eastern/East Indian.

W = White.

Additionally, SJPD uses letter codes to indicate the reasons for the stop based on four scenarios:

V– Victor. A violation of the California vehicle code.

P– Paul. A California penal code violation, e.g., an officer might have observed a person committing a criminal violation (picking up a known prostitute).

M– Mary. A municipal code violation.[40]

B– Boy. A notice or an all-points bulletin was broadcast on police radio channels, or a description of the suspect or car was issued in a report or bulletin by a police organization in the area.

Under both the pre-June vehicle-stop procedures and the new data collection system, the officer clears a call by indicating the disposition or outcome of the traffic-stop. The codes used for the stop disposition are as follows:

A = Arrest made.

B = Warrant arrest made.

C = Criminal citation issued.

D = Traffic citation issued—hazardous.

E = Traffic citation issued—nonhazardous.

F = Field interview card.

H = Courtesy service/assistance.

N = No report completed.[41]

Once the officer provides the information by computer or over the radio, it is relayed to an automated computer-aided dispatch system and automatically entered into a new database. By collecting the information immediately after each stop on an already existing system, SJPD is able to keep up-to-date accurate information on all vehicle stops.

Identifying and Overcoming Perceived Difficulties

Racial and ethnic designations. San Jose determined that because an officer's perceptions gives rise to the problem of racial profiling, the officer's perception is an appropriate means of ascertaining race or ethnicity. It seemed unimportant whether the officer had correctly guessed the race or ethnicity of the driver; what seemed important was to analyze whether, having perceived the driver as a person of color, the officer treated the person fairly.

Costs. SJPD opted for a simple system that kept the quantity of information low, so that data could be gathered quickly without tremendous financial costs. The additional time an officer needs to clear a call is less than 3 seconds. Moreover, the system costs less than $10,000, which includes the software for the existing 1990 system and training, training materials, and plastic pocket-size reference cards issued to each officer. It does not include the cost for data analysis.

Disengagement. Police disengagement from duty or any reduction in stops, searches, and arrests is a concern of many local jurisdictions. In San Jose, initial analysis indicates that the number of traffic-stops has increased rather than decreased.[42] Thus, San Jose does not appear to have experienced any disengagement.

Data integrity. San Jose employs only routine supervision of the data collection procedures. No systemic mechanism for spot-checking or cross-checking the data is currently in place.

Quantity of data. The San Jose system covers all traffic-stops. Ideally, an officer cannot clear a call and get back in service without providing the reason for the stop, the race of the driver, the outcome of the stop, and whether the driver was an adult or a minor. As designed, neither the dispatcher nor the computer will clear the call without this information.[43] However, the system does not record whether a search was conducted or the basis or results of the search. It also does not cover pedestrian stops. Finally, it only provides a list of four possible reasons for the stop: all-points bulletin, municipal code violation, penal code violation, or vehicle code violation.[44] The system fails to distinguish, for example, between a high-discretion stop for underinflated tires and a low-discretion stop for traveling 20 miles over the speed limit. Thus, while it provides a fast, simple, inexpensive means of obtaining data on stops, it may not provide sufficient information for a complete analysis of the problem. Still, the system deserves praise for its simplicity and ability to be adopted in jurisdictions without computerized facilities. San Jose is considering adding a code to indicate whether a search was conducted.[45] San Jose's dedication to a community-oriented response to the problem of racial profiling serves as a model for other police departments.

Officer resistance. Recognizing that officers might feel insulted about collecting data and resist the implementation of the system, Chief Lansdowne established an extensive training program focused on line officers. During training, officers were instructed to explain the reason for a traffic-stop to each driver and to be respectful and courteous during the entire encounter. Lansdowne stressed that developing traffic-stop protocols and implementing data collection systems were ways to enhance the professionalism of the department. He emphasized that San Jose's system did not require any additional written reports and it was a simpler and less onerous alternative to the proposed legislative model for data collection. The data collection system has received support and active input from members of the police officers' union.

Use of the data. To garner the support of the San Jose Police Officers' Association, the local police union, the identity of the citizen and the police officer involved in a stop must remain anonymous. Thus, the data will not be used to discipline or analyze the stops of individual officers but solely to evaluate the department on a systemwide basis.[46]

Data Analysis

On December 17, 1999, Chief Lansdowne issued SJPD's first preliminary analysis of the data collected from July 1 to September 30.[47] Although the study is ongoing, the preliminary report provides some initial analysis of the demographics of San Jose's traffic-stops.

To analyze the data, the department decided to compare the racial and ethnic demographics of those stopped with the racial and ethnic makeup of the residential population. Obtaining the residential demographics proved difficult. The demographics from the 1990 national census were criticized by many because the census failed to accurately count the minority population in many geographic areas.[48] Additionally, in 1995, the California Department of Finance issued some small-area race and ethnicity statistics. Thus, although actual statistics on the demographics of San Jose's residential population were unreliable, SJPD was able to use estimates from both the 1990 census and the 1995 California Department of Finance study to create a comparative residential population.[49]

Having created a residential benchmark population, SJPD then compared those population demographics with the demographics of their traffic-stops. Table 1 illustrates the results.

African Americans and Hispanics were stopped at a rate exceeding their percentage of the residential population. However, SJPD believes there are two reasons for this outcome: the number of officers per capita is concentrated in the police districts with more Hispanic and African-American populations, and socioeconomic factors in minority neighborhoods lead to more calls for service and interactions with police. Each factor is addressed below.

Table 1 Traffic Stops by Race

Race/Ethnicity	San Jose's Population (%)	Total Vehicle Stops (%)	Variation
African American	5%	7%	+2.0
Asian	21%	16%	−5.0
Hispanic	31%	43%	+12.0
White	43%	29%	−14.0

The number of officers per capita in smaller minority police districts. San Jose is made up of 16 police districts, each of which was created by using a computer model that allowed for the calls for police services to be spread out evenly among all districts. As a result, in areas where residents' 911 calls for police service per capita are higher, the geographic size of a district is smaller. These small districts, however, have the same number of officers assigned to them as larger geographic districts. Since the number of calls for police services is higher in minority neighborhoods, the number of officers per capita is concentrated in these small districts. SJPD examined traffic-stops by district and found that the percentage of stops by the police closely mirrors the racial population of these districts. These are only impressions since SJPD does not have the racial population percentages for individual police districts.

Socioeconomic factors that lead to more interactions with police. Other factors that may lead to more interactions with the police include social problems such as unemployment and poverty rates. SJPD suggests that these factors may lead to more stops being made on vehicles that have not been properly maintained.[50]

SJPD's preliminary report indicates that, although Hispanics and African Americans are stopped at rates higher than their percentage of the residential population, this overrepresentation may be explained when compared to other law enforcement-related data and statistics. However, using residential population statistics does not capture the racial demographics of the roadways in that both residents and nonresidents drive on the roadways. Additionally, the residential population data used in San Jose were not limited to the segment of the population that is within the legal driving age. Finally, the San Jose population statistics cannot account for differences in the driving behavior of individuals of different racial groups, if such differences exist. These concerns illustrate the need for additional research to refine the data analysis process.

Lessons Learned and Future Suggestions

Chief Lansdowne believes that a data collection system should be simple and not require officers to prepare additional written reports. Obtaining the police union's support enabled the system to be implemented smoothly. Informing officers about the need for data collection encouraged officers to accept the new system. Once training was completed, educating the media about the process became a critical activity for SJPD. SJPD would like to equip all of its cars with video cameras, which would contextualize the data collection process.[51] In addition, cameras might change the nature of police-citizen encounters because when parties know that their behavior is being recorded, both police and civilians are more likely to be on their best behavior. However, due to the high costs associated with installing video cameras, SJPD has not used video monitoring on a systemwide basis.

The San Diego Experience

San Diego, the nation's seventh largest city, has its share of crime problems. The San Diego Police Department (SDPD) routinely deals with violence along the border with Mexico and the drugs that travel across it. Its population is diverse, with a Hispanic community that comprises 23.2 percent of the population and sizable Black (8.8 percent) and Asian (5 percent) populations. It is one of the most lightly policed major cities in the United States. Only 2,683 police officers serve its population of roughly 1.25 million.[52]

The city of San Diego has enjoyed remarkable success in reducing crime, which has declined for 9 consecutive years. Since 1991, its homicide rate has declined 75 percent.[53] The city's style of policing emphasizes strong community bonds and relationships, assisted by 1,100 civilian volunteers who donate about 200,000 hours of service annually.[54] In 1998, SDPD made about 200,000 vehicle stops, issuing citations in 125,000 of these stops.[55]

In February 1999, SDPD became the first big-city police department in the nation to voluntarily record the racial and ethnic demographics of its traffic-stops to determine whether minority motorists were being pulled over at a higher rate than White drivers.[56]

Precipitating Events

As in other cities, for years local community groups complained that police were disproportionately stopping people of color for minor traffic offenses.[57] The perception that SDPD was using race as a basis for conducting traffic-stops was fueled by an incident in 1997. While driving his Jeep Cherokee, San Diego Chargers football player Shawn Lee was pulled over by the police because he was thought to be driving a vehicle that fit the description of a car stolen earlier that evening. Lee and his girlfriend were handcuffed and detained for half an hour. Later, however, the *San Diego Union Tribune* reported that the stolen vehicle had been, in fact, a Honda sedan.[58]

Former San Diego Police Chief Jerry Sanders recognized that the perception that police were engaged in racial profiling needed to be addressed if community policing was going to continue to be successful. Like other California police chiefs, he was aware that legislation was pending in the California legislature that would require state law enforcement agencies to begin tracking the race and ethnicity of motorists stopped for routine traffic violations.

During a meeting with Chief Sanders in July 1998, local African American leaders raised their concerns about racial profiling. In February 1999, Sanders met with leaders of the local ACLU, Urban League, National Association for the Advancement of Colored People, and Human Relations Commission who asked him to begin collecting data on all traffic-stops. He agreed to do so if it was not too costly. By March 1999, it was clear that data collection would be technically feasible and that the costs would not be excessive. Sanders announced his decision to collect the requested data.

When questioned about the initiative, Sanders said that he was not afraid of what the data might reveal and reiterated that he believed the police were doing their job professionally. However, he felt data collection was necessary to allay community perceptions about profiling and to retain SDPD's credibility and trust with the community. He told the press, "This perception [of racial profiling], whether true or not, is eroding public trust and needs to be addressed."[59]

Data Collection Process

SDPD began collecting traffic-stop data in January 2000. Each of its 1,300 patrol, traffic, and canine officers has been issued a laptop computer that they can use inside or outside their patrol cars to enter data.[60] In addition, SDPD has 45 motorcycle officers who write about 50 percent of all traffic citations. These officers use wireless handheld computers to collect data.

San Diego's data collection program focuses on all traffic-stops, regardless of whether a citation or warning is issued. To tally the racial demographics of the traffic-stops in San Diego, SDPD decided to focus on 14 basic data elements:

❑ District.

❑ Date and time.

❑ Cause for stop—moving violation, equipment violation, radio call/citizen complaint, personal observation/knowledge, suspect info (e.g., bulletin, log), or municipal/county code violation.

❑ Race.

❑ Gender.

❑ Age.

❑ Disposition of the stop—citation issued, oral warning, written warning, field interview, or other.

❑ Arrest (yes/no).

❑ Search (yes/no).

❑ Search type—vehicle, driver, or passengers.

❑ Basis for search—contraband visible, odor of contraband, canine alert, inventory search prior to impound, consent search, 4th waiver search, search incident to arrest, inventory search, observed evidence related to criminal activity, or other.

❑ Obtained consent search form (yes/no).

❑ Contraband found (yes/no).

❑ Property seized (yes/no).

These elements provide the information that would have been required in the 1999 California Traffic-stop Data Collection legislation, except San Diego elected not to collect information on the nature and amount of contraband discovered during a search.

In San Diego, an officer who makes a traffic-stop advises the radio communications dispatcher of the stop and its location. Next, the officer runs the car's license plate. The officer talks to the driver, asks for a license and registration, and goes back to the patrol car to make a decision on disposition. The officer informs the driver of the disposition and then completes the data entry form on the laptop or handheld computer. As a fail-safe procedure, officers must complete the forms before the dispatcher clears the call and allows the officer back in service.

Identifying and Overcoming Perceived Difficulties

Racial and ethnic designations and categories. San Diego decided to use the officer's perception of the driver's race or ethnicity for its data collection program. If unsure, the officer may ask the driver. Because community groups had complained that officers treated drivers differently because of the way they perceived their race or ethnicity, the use of "officer perception" seemed appropriate. Current Police Chief David Bejarano thought that asking drivers about their race might exacerbate the community's perception that racial profiling was occurring and that many officers may not feel comfortable asking motorists their race.

The department uses the following racial categories on its incident reports:

A = Other Asian.	K = Korean.
B = Black.	L = Laotian.
C = Chinese.	O = Other.
D = Cambodian.	P = Pacific Islander.
F = Filipino.	S = Samoan.
G = Guamanian.	U = Hawaiian.
H = Hispanic.	V = Vietnamese.
I = Indian.	W = White.
J = Japanese.	Z = Asian Indian.

Cost. For SDPD, the system was relatively easy to implement because it was able to use a previously installed in-house data system. Since all patrol cars had a mobile dispatch terminal and each officer already had a laptop, the hardware costs were minimal. Because the department's computer software was already designed in a Windows environment, it was able to use Microsoft Access to develop a series of pulldown menus for each of the 14 data collection elements. The department developed its own in-house software, so there were no costs for programming. The data services department estimates that it will need two additional computer servers, bringing the data collection costs to approximately $30,000.[61]

It is estimated that it will take officers an additional 20 to 30 seconds to enter the data by making choices on the computer pulldown menus. Since most traffic-stops do not result in a search, officers will be completing only the first seven elements. The other elements will default to "no."

Disengagement. According to former Chief Sanders, disengagement was not a primary concern when adopting the data collection system. He did not believe that traffic-stops constitute an essential police enforcement activity. Sanders stated, "The officers should be out on the street working to prevent gang activity, getting to know the community, and helping to decrease truancy by making sure kids are in school. I never emphasized traffic enforcement as a primary activity. In fact, during my tenure, traffic-stops decreased more than 50 percent because I diverted my officers to other more important activities, and during that time, crime continued to go down despite a less aggressive 'traffic-stop' policy. Of course, my officers always enforced hazardous driving infractions such as excessive speeding or running a red light, but the vehicle equipment violations and failure to signal incidents were not high on my enforcement agenda."[62]

Consequently, in San Diego, disengagement was not viewed as a major concern, given the relative importance of traffic-stop enforcement versus other enforcement priorities. Former Chief Sanders explained that community policing meetings can be a better use of resources than random traffic-stop procedures.

Data integrity. Officials in San Diego felt that, if they instituted a mechanism to establish multiple sources of information so that the data could be cross-checked through random or automated procedures, the police union would oppose the data collection effort. Therefore, there is no independent mechanism for checking the data's accuracy. Instead, traffic and patrol supervisors are responsible for ensuring that officers properly record and enter traffic-stop data. In addition, to enter the data in the computer, officers must also enter the information in their daily journals. Officers have been informed that entering information that the officer knows to be false is a violation of departmental policies that could result in disciplinary action.

Quantity of data. SDPD elected to cover only traffic-stops. Since pedestrian stops constitute a significant percentage of all police-civilian stops, the analysis will focus on only one aspect of the potential problem. San Diego's data collection system will provide information on stops and searches, but it will not qualify or quantify the nature of contraband seized during a search.

Officer resistance. When former Chief Sanders announced his decision to collect data, some traffic officers said that they were insulted by the idea that they made traffic-stops based on a person's race.[63] Although the idea of the data collection system was generally well received, according to current Police Chief Bejarano, about 10 percent of the officers expressed concerns about the system. Some of those concerns included the following:

❑ Would there be disciplinary activities associated with this data collection process?

❑ Would it apply to specialized units?

❑ Would there be fewer traffic-stops because officers feared being monitored for stopping too many minorities?

❑ Would officers be labeled "racists" if their traffic-stop patterns indicated they were stopping a disproportionate number of minorities?

To allay these fears, SDPD undertook an extensive training program to explain to officers the purposes of the program, the nature and extent of community perceptions, how the data would be analyzed, and how the program would affect each officer. The department chose not to include officer identification in the stop-and-search data collection system.

In addition to the data collection system training, officers were instructed to be courteous and tell drivers the reason for the stop. Sergeant Tony McElroy was put in charge of this training. He involved firstline supervisors in the process, was available during training sessions, and gave out his phone number so that officers could talk to him privately about their concerns.

Use of the data. SDPD has ensured that, during the data collection process, neither the officer nor the motorist will be identified by name. The data will only be collected, used, and analyzed in the aggregate. The identification of officers was omitted from the data collection process to assure officers that data collection was to assess whether the department as a whole was acting professionally, rather than to isolate or punish individual conduct.

Data Analysis

San Diego plans to analyze the data by divisions, of which there are eight. Analysts fear a citywide analysis would not produce an accurate picture of police enforcement patterns, which vary by neighborhood. The department is struggling with how to create a comparative statistical measure and is not certain about how to calculate a potential violator population for each of the eight districts. However, the department is working with academic partners from the University of California at San Diego, University of San Diego, and San Diego State to develop appropriate benchmarks.

The North Carolina Experience

North Carolina is a state with both rural areas and medium-size metropolitan cities. Based on the 1990 census, North Carolina's population of 6.5 million is approximately 75.6 percent White, 22.2 percent Black, and 2.2 percent other racial groups.[64] The North Carolina Highway Patrol (NCHP) is the state's primary law enforcement organization and consists of 1,417 troopers and a 12-member interdiction team. Troopers patrol interstate highways and local roads. Last year, NCHP issued 684,721 traffic citations.[65]

Precipitating Events

For years, Black drivers in North Carolina complained that they were routinely stopped on flimsy pretexts and were subsequently questioned and searched for drugs far more often than White drivers.[66] On July 28, 1996, the *Raleigh News and Observer* reported that NCHP's drug interdiction team stopped and charged Black male drivers at nearly twice the rate of other troopers patrolling those same roads.[67] Subsequently, the newspaper reported that, based on 1998 statistics, Blacks and other minorities were twice as likely as White drivers to have their cars searched by the drug unit.[68]

In 1999, State Senator Frank Balance and State Representative Ronnie Sutton, working with the local ACLU office, introduced a bill requiring state law enforcement entities to collect data on all routine traffic-stops. On April 22, 1999, North Carolina became the first state to enact such a law.[69]

Data Collection Process

The data collection system is designed to be statewide and apply to all traffic-stops by any state police organization. Although NCHP is the largest state law enforcement entity, the data collection law applies to other state law enforcement organizations such as the Department of Fish and Wildlife and the State University Police. NCHP began collecting traffic-stop data on January 1, 2000. The data are collected in real time using a computerized system. Each trooper's car has an MDT, allowing the trooper to enter data on the stop. The trooper uses Access, a Windows-based software system, to record the required data. Using pulldown menus, each trooper completes the form electronically.

Under the law, state troopers are required to specify the race, age, and gender of every driver and passenger they stop, regardless of whether the occupants were arrested, cited, warned, or sent on their way. The law applies to all traffic-stops but not to pedestrian stops. It is one of the most comprehensive data collection laws, requiring troopers to collect the following data:

❑ The initial reason for the stop.

❑ The identifying characteristics of the drivers stopped, including race/ethnicity, gender, and approximate age.

❑ The type of enforcement action, if any, that was taken as a result of the stop.

❑ Whether any physical resistance was encountered.

❑ Whether a search was conducted.

Troopers rarely conduct searches, but if one occurs, the following additional information must be recorded:

❑ Type of search.

❑ Basis for the search.

❑ Whether vehicle, driver, or passengers were searched.

❑ Race/ethnicity and gender of those searched.

❑ A description of the contraband found and whether any property was seized.

Identifying and Overcoming Perceived Difficulties

Racial and ethnic designation and categories. Race and ethnicity data are collected as separate variables. Troopers designate White, Black, Indian, Asian, or other as the racial categories and Hispanic or non-Hispanic as the ethnic categories. Currently, the plan is that troopers will use their best judgement regarding the race and ethnicity utilizing either:

- Perception of the person after the traffic-stop encounter.
- Information provided by the driver of the vehicle.
- Backup racial and ethnic information collected by the Bureau of Motor Vehicles.[70]

Time burdens and financial costs. The time required to complete the form electronically is expected to be less than 5 minutes. NCHP Colonel Richard Holden believes this is not a significant burden. He stated, "How much is 5 minutes when it means stopping the perception that exists about police misbehavior? It is not much time to ask out of an officer's day."[71]

It cost NCHP $50,000 to implement this system, including the costs of a new computer server, hardware, and software. This cost excludes equipping each cruiser with an MDT unit. The software was developed with the help of the International Association of Chiefs of Police. Equipping all the cruisers with MDT units costs $8,000 per car. The units are being used for various purposes in addition to data collection. NCHP, for independent reasons, would have begun to equip each cruiser with an MDT unit, even without the data collection legislation.[72]

Disengagement. Prior to passage of the data collection law, NCHP collected racial data only on the number of written citations and warnings. The department did not collect any reliable information about traffic-stops resulting in verbal warnings.[73] Consequently, it may be difficult to gauge whether troopers stop fewer cars as a result of the new data collection system.

Data integrity. Currently, there is no plan to audit or verify the data independently or to engage in systematic cross-checking procedures.

Officer resistance. At first, some troopers were insulted by the suggestion that they were engaging in racist behavior. Colonel Holden met with troopers across the state to explain the goals of the data collection process and the department's commitment to fully participate in this effort. Once the data protocol was finalized, training workshops were provided to all troopers. As part of the training, Colonel Holden emphasized that the data would not be used for discipline of individual officers and expressed his hope that collecting the data would improve the training and performance of all the troopers. He said that the process can be used to understand and improve practices for NCHP.

Data Analysis

NCHP will not collect individual officer identification numbers. Consequently, the department plans to use the data to assess the prevalence of any systemwide problems in traffic-stops. Preliminary reports of traffic-stop data for January 2000 indicate that Black motorists were stopped in proportion to their representation in the state population.[74] However,

Black motorists were disproportionally searched and arrested when compared with their percentage of the state population.

In addition to releasing monthly aggregate statistics for traffic-stops, NCHP is working with Professor Matthew Zingraff, associate dean at the Center for Crime and Justice Research, North Carolina State University. With the help of a National Institute of Justice grant, Zingraff is trying to identify a statistical benchmark that will enable him to compare the relevant violator population with the data from highway patrol stops. He is trying to identify the population at risk of being stopped in selected geographic areas. Since he cannot quantify the risk of being stopped for weaving, reckless driving, or following too closely, he will focus on the risk of being stopped for speeding. Having mapped certain segments of the interstates, he plans to identify the racial/ethnic demographics of an "at-risk" population by having troopers certified in the use of radar guns and two observers parked in stationary locations. The troopers will identify cars travelling in excess of 8 miles above the speed limit. Observers in the car will identify the race/ethnicity, age, and gender of the drivers (these will be estimates).

Another possibility is a "rolling carousel" model in which the researchers move with traffic. Again, troopers will have mounted radar guns concealed by tinted windshields and will identify the demographics of drivers traveling in excess of 8 miles above the speed limit.

Zingraff's study will help create a baseline against which to measure NCHP enforcement patterns. He also plans to conduct a survey asking citizens to describe their "perceived safe driving speed," that is, the speed at which they believe they can safely travel without being stopped.

Quantity of Data

North Carolina's data collection system is comprehensive. When a trooper indicates the initial reason for a stop, the data collection form creates separate categories for moving violations, speeding violations, vehicle equipment violations, and so on. This design enables NCHP to analyze high-discretion vehicle equipment stops separately from low-discretion stops for excessive speed and hazardous moving violations. It focuses only on traffic-stops, and it captures information about searches.

Collecting information about the duration and location of the stop might further enrich the ultimate analysis. Some members of NCHP believe cameras in patrol cars would be a useful adjunct to the data collection system. One of the problems with data collection is that it fails to provide a context for the stop. Adding cameras to a data collection system would provide a comprehensive integrated system.

The New Jersey Experience

New Jersey is a diverse eastern state with both medium-size cities and rural populations. Department of Labor and Management population demographic estimates for 1998 indicate that 79.4 percent of the state population is White, 15 percent is Black, and 4.2 percent is other racial groups.[75] The New Jersey State Police (NJSP) is the state's primary state law enforcement organization, with approximately 2,800 troopers. NJSP is 14 percent minority and 3 percent women. Troopers patrol both interstate highways and local roads and serve as the police force for approximately 50 rural jurisdictions.[76]

Precipitating Events

Allegations of racial profiling on the New Jersey state highways resulted in federal intervention. As a result of this intervention, the state of New Jersey and the U.S. Department of Justice reached a consent decree that included provisions for traffic-stop data collection and monitoring. The events leading up to the decree showed patterns of early warning signals of potential problems within NJSP.

The issue of racial profiling came to the public forefront more than a decade ago. In 1989, WWOR–TV Channel 9 carried a special segment titled "Without Just Cause" that highlighted the problem of racial profiling on highways in New Jersey. The investigative team surveyed tickets from the New Jersey Turnpike, interviewed drivers, and concluded that a disproportionate number of people ticketed on the turnpike were drivers of color. During this report, the investigative team presented interviews with state troopers who admitted that race was a factor in selecting which drivers to stop.[77] In 1996, a New Jersey Superior Court judge dismissed a case against 19 defendants following a motion to suppress evidence obtained in a series of searches, alleging that the searches were unlawful because they were part of a pattern and practice of racial profiling by the troopers.[78] As part of this litigation, Dr. John Lamberth testified that Blacks comprised 13.5 percent of the drivers on the southern portion of the turnpike and 15 percent of the drivers speeding. In contrast, Blacks represented 35 percent of those stopped. The court found that the defendants were unlawfully stopped and evidence presented against them was the result of an unlawful seizure.[79]

While this case was on appeal, on April 23, 1998, two troopers fired 11 shots into a van carrying 4 young Black males after a traffic-stop. Three of the young men were injured during the shooting.[80] Former State Police Superintendent Carl Williams reported that the van was pulled over because radar showed that the driver was speeding. However, later reports confirmed that the police patrol car was not equipped with a radar unit. Following the shooting, the two officers were brought before a state grand jury on charges of attempted murder and indicted for falsifying records to conceal the race of people they stopped and searched. In the months following the shooting, Governor Christine Whitman announced plans to secure funding for video cameras in police cars.

Attention to the issue of racial profiling peaked in February 1999 when the *Newark Star-Ledger* released statistics obtained from the state police documenting that three out of four motorists arrested on the turnpike in 2 selected months during 1997 were minorities.[81] Later that year, the newspaper published additional data for 1997 showing that four in five drivers arrested were minorities.[82] One dramatic illustration of the problem of racial profiling came during a *Star-Ledger* interview with then-NJSP Superintendent Williams, in which he explained, "The drug problem is cocaine or marijuana. It is most likely a minority group that is involved with that."[83] Governor Whitman fired Superintendent Williams shortly after this public statement.

On April 20, 1999, then-Acting New Jersey Attorney General Peter Verniero issued a 112-page report acknowledging the potential problems of racial profiling within the NJSP.[84] The attorney general's report recommended several internal reforms including an early warning system to detect patterns of discrimination by individual troopers or particular interdiction units. Facing a potential federal civil rights suit for racial bias in police stops and searches, New Jersey entered into a consent decree with DOJ mandating traffic-stop-and-search data collection.[85]

Data Collection Process

Pursuant to the federal consent decree, NJSP began gathering traffic-stop data on May 1, 2000. The data collection system is designed for use by state troopers engaged in patrol activities.[86] The initial data collection protocol relies on using the existing computer aided dispatch (CAD) system. Under this system, officers report the following information to the CAD operator:

- ❑ Name and identification number of all troopers who actively participated in the stop.

- ❑ Location, date, and time at which the stop commenced and ended.

- ❑ License plate number and state in which the car is registered.

- ❑ Description of the vehicle.

- ❑ Gender, race/ethnicity of the driver and date of birth of the driver (if known).

- ❑ Gender and race/ethnicity of any passengers.

- ❑ Whether the driver was issued a summons or warning and the category of violation (i.e., moving violation or nonmoving violation).

- ❑ Reason for the stop (i.e., moving violation, nonmoving violation, or probable cause).

The consent decree specifies that officers should make initial calls to the communication center before approaching the car, unless circumstances make this practice unsafe or impractical. CAD operators will manually enter data transmitted by troopers at the time of each stop. Eventually, NJSP plans to place laptops in all patrol cars, allowing officers to enter the traffic-stop data directly. At the end of the call, the communication center assigns an incident number to each motor vehicle stop. This number can be used to track information about poststop enforcement actions and can be useful in future auditing mechanisms.

The consent decree also specifies that troopers should notify the communications center prior to conducting searches. Any poststop enforcement action is recorded on a Motor Vehicle Stop Report (MVSR) for those traffic-stops in which the officer orders an occupant out of his or her vehicle, requests a consent search, conducts a search, requests a drug-detection canine, frisks an occupant, makes an arrest, recovers contraband or other property, or uses force. This additional stop report includes the race, gender, and date of birth of the occupants and an explanation concerning the process when one of these eight procedures is invoked.

Identifying and Overcoming Perceived Difficulties

Racial and ethnic designations and categories. The traffic-stop data collection uses the following racial/ethnic categories:

- ❑ White.
- ❑ Black.
- ❑ Hispanic/Latino.
- ❑ Asian Indian (Asian subcontinent, e.g., India, Pakistan).
- ❑ Other Asian.
- ❑ American Indian/Native American.

In New Jersey, troopers do not ask drivers to identify their race or ethnicity. Instead, officers rely on their perceptions to provide the racial/ethnic data.

Time burdens and financial costs. Although the state has not conducted a formal study concerning the additional radio transmission time, it is anticipated that little additional time will be required by troopers to relay the data collection information over the CAD system. The attorney general's office estimates that it will take several minutes for an officer to fill out the additional information on MVSR forms. However, poststop enforcement activities make up only a small percentage of an officer's daily duties.

The costs of such a wide-reaching, comprehensive data collection system are high. The state estimates that the modifications for the CAD system will cost $130,000. Also, the attorney general's office has estimated that

$1.43 million will be spent on officer training. The training is designed to educate troopers about the data collection protocol and provides substantial additional training on criminal procedure and search and seizure law. Also, $12.581 million is budgeted for the purchase and installation of mobile video recorders and mobile data computers.

Disengagement. NJSP expressed concerns about officer disengagement. The attorney general's office reports that patrol-related arrests have decreased dramatically since the state began implementing its revised patrol practices and data collection system.[87] The reason for disengagement is currently under review. Because the consent decree was not implemented until May 2000, and the disengagement began much earlier, other factors such as the ongoing investigation of trooper misconduct may be responsible for the disengagement.

Data integrity. Under the terms of the federal consent decree, the attorney general is responsible for auditing the traffic-stop data for accuracy. The attorney general's office is required to contact a sampling of persons who were the stopped by troopers to evaluate whether the stops were appropriately conducted and documented.[88] Additionally, the decree specifies that supervisors will regularly review trooper reports on poststop enforcement actions and videotapes of traffic-stops to ensure accuracy of the information and the appropriateness of their actions.

Officer resistance. The publication of data was a primary concern of troopers. In the light of the tense political atmosphere around racial profiling and negative reports of officer behavior in the press, troopers expressed strong concerns that individual behavior would be reported to the press and that they would be labeled as racists.

Additionally, troopers raised concerns about the reliability of the CAD system and CAD officers. They feared that, if the CAD operators were short staffed, not trained, or inaccurate, the potential existed for misreporting traffic-stop data. The attorney general responded by hiring more CAD operators and adding training for troopers on the CAD system.

Data Analysis

The data from the New Jersey traffic studies will be collected and analyzed by individual officer identification numbers. This process allows the state attorney general to monitor both the prevalence of any systemwide problems in traffic-stops and flag individual officers who may be engaging in discriminatory traffic-stop practices. The data will be made available to both the state and an outside federal monitor.

Under the terms of the decree, NJSP will issue semiannual reports containing aggregate statistics on law enforcement activities.[89] These reports will include traffic-stop statistics. Attorney General Farmer explained that aggregate numbers alone would not dictate disciplinary action: "What we tried to move away from with the Justice Department was the idea that numbers alone dictate results. If it were the case that an officer had some proportion of a certain kind of stops, that would not trigger a conclusion of any kind; rather, it would trigger further investigation. So the numbers don't dictate results, they raise a red flag that we then pursue to see if there is a problem."[90]

The New Jersey Department of Law and Public Safety, in conjunction with DOJ, is conducting a survey of persons and vehicles traveling on the New Jersey Turnpike. The survey is designed to develop an objective sample of certain characteristics of persons and vehicles that travel on the turnpike. This traffic survey will serve as a tool to help the attorney general and other monitors determine whether an officer's stop patterns are disproportionate. At this time, the state has no plans to conduct an additional survey of the demographics of traffic violators on state highways.

Quantity of Data

New Jersey's data collection system captures a large amount of information, including detailed information on consent searches and the use of canines. However, the state police data collection system focuses only on traffic-stops, not pedestrian stops. Additionally, NJSP hopes to equip all trooper cars with video cameras by February 2001.

Lessons Learned

Collecting traffic-stop data is compatible with officer safety. Attorney General Farmer explained: "From our perspective, the fundamental point that we would want to communicate to others, and that I have said to several other of my colleagues, is that addressing this issue is not incompatible with promoting officer safety, or robbing law enforcement of its efficacy. When you make people accountable, who basically haven't been in the past because of antiquated record keeping and because of an institutional culture that didn't promote openness, of course there is a reaction and a recoiling."

Additionally, the New Jersey experience shows that allegations of racial profiling may be part of larger structural or organizational problems within a police organization. For example, in New Jersey, the state police were trained and rewarded for high numbers of arrests, as opposed to making quality arrests.[91] In addition to contributing to allegations of racial profiling, this emphasis may have undermined the effectiveness of police practices. In an interim report, the attorney general acknowledges two primary concerns: documented stop-and-search practices producing a "find" rate of only 10 percent were ineffective, and the find rates did not vary across races. Attorney General Farmer illustrated the costs of such ineffective policing. He explained that, during a recent highway drug interdiction program on the turnpike, an investigative team interdicted a tractor-trailer carrying approximately $1 million in contraband. This interdiction was supported with intelligence, wiretaps, and specific targets. Conversely, the attorney general explained, the nearly 500 seizures from traffic-stops in 1999 netted only $60,000 in contraband, illustrating the ineffectiveness of traffic "profiling" for high-level drug interdiction.

According to Attorney General Farmer, addressing the problem of profiling is just one piece of a much larger program of restructuring within NJSP. The traffic-stop data collection system is one critical part of its new effective management strategy.

The Experience in Great Britain

Currently, data collection on the racial and ethnic demographics of police searches is occurring throughout England and Wales, a region that includes a mixture of urban and rural areas. The largest urban center is London, with a population of 7 million. Great Britain is 81 percent White, 7.5 percent Black, 7.3 percent Asian, and 4.2 percent other.[92]

In London, the Metropolitan Police Service (MPS) numbers 26,000, plus a civilian staff of 15,000. The current MPS program to monitor the race and ethnicity of persons searched and (in seven pilot sites) stopped by police officers was developed after a period of racial unrest in the 1970s and early 1980s. Authorities within the British Government, concerned about increasing claims that police were disproportionally stopping and searching ethnic minorities, determined that a systematic data collection system was necessary to address questions about police legitimacy and ethnic bias. In 1991, the Criminal Justice Act was passed requiring the home secretary to publish "such information necessary to assess the existence of racial discrimination in police practices." The original program of ethnic monitoring required data collection on searches, arrests, cautions, and homicides.[93]

Precipitating Events: The Stephen Lawrence Murder and the MacPherson Report

Several high-profile events led MPS to expand the scope of race and ethnicity data collection required under the Criminal Justice Act of 1991. On April 22, 1993, in the southeastern London suburb of Elthram, two young Black men, Stephen Lawrence and Duwayne Brooks, were rushing to catch a bus when they were confronted by a gang of White youths. The gang, who did not know Lawrence, attacked him with knives. After being badly beaten, he managed to scramble free but was bleeding profusely. After 200 yards, he collapsed and died.[94]

The subsequent police investigation, or lack of investigation, of this hate crime sparked a long protest and inquiry. Although an inquest verdict indicated that Lawrence was killed in a completely unprovoked racist attack by five White youths, none of them was ever convicted.[95] MPS's investigation of the Lawrence murder was severely criticized as flawed by corruption, incompetence, and racism.[96] A subsequent private prosecution ended in an acquittal. In July 1997, the home secretary announced in Parliament that an investigation of Lawrence's murder would be undertaken,[97] and Sir William MacPherson was asked to chair the public inquiry into the murder. Released in 1999, the *MacPherson Report* criticized MSP for "institutionally racist" practices.

The report's recommendations dealt not only with the investigation and prosecution of hate crimes but also with the general problems and differing perceptions that exist between the minority ethnic communities and the police.[98] During the public inquiry, there were universal complaints from the minority community that police discriminate in the practice of stopping and searching civilians.[99] In his report, MacPherson recommended that police officers record, monitor, and analyze the racial and ethnic demographics of all police stops and searches.[100]

The Stephen Lawrence case and the MacPherson public inquiry and report were widely covered in the press, and these events were critical catalysts to Great Britain's current data collection efforts. In 1998, MPS began pilot data collection programs in seven jurisdictions.[101]

Data Collection Process

For the last 3 years, all police departments in Great Britain have been collecting data on all Police and Criminal Evidence (PACE) Act searches.[102] PACE provides British police with the power to stop-and-search any person or vehicle when the officer has reasonable grounds for suspecting that stolen or prohibited articles will be found.[103] While these vehicle and pedestrian stops may seem equivalent to the American stop-and-frisk practice, PACE powers are actually quite different: they allow officers to conduct a full search, as opposed to a mere pat down of outer clothing, for weapons. Consequently, police officers can conduct a full search of the person, as well as anything they may be carrying or any vehicle they are in.

While the current British data collection system records information on all PACE pedestrian and vehicle searches, it does not include PACE stops that do not result in a search or on-PACE stops and searches such as traffic-stops or voluntary stops. However, selected pilot locations have tested data collection programs collecting information on all police stops.[104]

Data collection mechanism. Police are using paper forms to collect the data. Each officer carries an Information for Persons Searched form, which the officer completes after a search has been conducted. The form consists of a yellow face sheet and a white carbon copy. Individuals searched are entitled to a full copy of the record of the search (the white copy) at the time of the search or, upon demand, within 12 months. Since the process of completing the form may take 5 to 10 minutes, most people do not wait for the officer to complete the form.

Elements collected. After each search, police record the reason for the search; information about the person searched; a description of the person or vehicle searched; the location, date, and time of the stop; and the object and grounds for the search.

On the search form, police specify the grounds for the search as follows:

❑ Reasonable grounds exist to search for stolen property or offensive weapons.

❑ Reasonable grounds exist to search for drugs.

❑ Reasonable grounds exist to search for firearms.

❑ Reasonable grounds exist to search for certain dangerous weapons.

❑ A senior officer authorized searches in particular circumstances without reasonable grounds.[105]

❑ Terrorism searches are conducted.

Next, officers complete information about the person searched including name, address, date of birth, and telephone number. They describe the person searched including their clothing, height, and gender. The form asks whether clothing was searched or intimate parts exposed. The fourth section gathers information about the vehicle searched and whether property was found. A description of property found is required. Finally, the time, date, and location of the search are recorded. A separate line indicates whether the person was arrested.

Identifying and Overcoming Potential Difficulties

Racial and ethnic designations. Police have been using the following racial and ethnic categories:

❑ White-skinned European appearance, e.g., English, Scottish, Welsh, French, German, Swedish, Norwegian, Polish, and Russian.

❑ Dark-skinned European appearance, e.g., Mediterranean, Greek, Turkish, Sicilian, Sardinian, Spanish, and Italian.

❑ Black.

❑ Asian.

Police categorize persons searched based on the officer's perception. Initially, it was deemed impractical to ask individuals about their racial and/or ethnic background. However, the McPherson report specifically recommended that, when an officer records information about stops and searches, the records include the reason for the stop, the outcome, and the self-identified ethnic identity of the person, in addition to a description of the person. Consequently, police will begin asking the person to self-identify using one of 17 self-identification categories:

1. White–Northern Europe.
2. White–Southern Europe.
3. White–other.
4. Black–British.
5. Black–Caribbean.
6. Black–African.
7. Black–other.
8. Asian–Indian.
9. Pakistani.
10. Bangladeshi.
11. Chinese.
12. Asian–other.
13. Arabic.
14. Other.
15. Mixed Origin–Black/White.
16. Mixed Origin–Asian/White.
17. Mixed Origin–Other.[106]

Costs. Searching is a relatively rare activity for British police officers. During an interview, one officer in Hounslow estimated that on any given day, less than 5 percent of his time involves searches. The search form itself takes 5 to 10 minutes to complete. In Hounslow, where they are completing forms on all stops and searches on an experimental basis, an officer can complete the stop portion of the form in approximately 2 minutes. Since the English system records data on paper, each police district pays for data entry, at an approximate cost of $8,000 per year.

Disengagement. Beginning in 1998, the official philosophy underlying searches changed. The new philosophy emphasized the quality rather than the quantity of searches.[107] This change meant focusing on the percentage of searches that resulted in arrests for serious offenses. As a result, the search productivity and arrest rates have improved.[108] Thus, by late 1999, in selected pilot sites, the proportion of recorded searches for which an arrest had also been recorded had gradually risen.[109] More recent figures demonstrate that the trend has been sustained. From 1998 to 1999, the arrest rate across the MPS force was 17 percent.[110]

An analysis of search records indicates that most of the searches conducted by police are high-discretion or proactive searches rather than low-discretion searches driven by information given to police from other sources.[111] The overall fall in searches has been far more marked with respect to high-discretion searches.[112]

However, the volume of arrests has decreased. Indeed, the overall number of arrests and searches has dropped by nearly 33 percent among the selected pilot sites.[113] Marian FitzGerald, a researcher who has studied this phenomenon, attributes the decrease in searches to the ongoing McPherson inquiry, as well as a reduced police presence on the streets.[114] Officers interviewed expressed a deep loss of morale that has influenced the effectiveness of MPS during and after the McPherson inquiry. FitzGerald reports, "Many officers felt a deep sense of personal injustice, perceiving their integrity systematically and relentlessly being called into question and believing they each stood indicted individually of institutional racism."[115] A number of events that required high-profile policing took 60 percent more officers in London away from normal street duties, so fewer officers were available to undertake routine searches. Also, during 1998 and 1999 fewer officers were on the street.[116] These factors indicate that, although there has been disengagement, a number of exogenous factors may account for the decrease in PACE searches.

Quantity of data. Currently, other than in the seven pilot sites, police only collect data on PACE searches. Their data collection system will become broader when they begin to record all stops, regardless of whether the stop results in a search or an arrest. As noted earlier, once data collection is expanded to include all stops, a richer analysis of England's stop-and-search policy can occur.

Officer resistance. As noted earlier, many officers feel frustrated by mounting paperwork and the barriers that constrain their professional judgment. Only part of this frustration is due to PACE data collection. In England, few officers have access to a computer, so most of their information processes require completion of paper forms.

Use of the data and analysis. The Information from Persons Searched forms are used to monitor, supervise, and discipline individual officers. The name and signature of the officer conducting the search is on the form. By collecting this information, police are able to identify officers engaging in "best practices" as well as officers whose search patterns seem questionable.

All analysis conducted on the British data has been based on residential population figures. Analysts have not yet developed a system for calculating a comparative benchmark that would incorporate differing criminal participation rates. This comparative population might differ from residential statistics because many individuals who are searched do not live in the neighborhood where the search occurred.

Lessons learned. Three important lessons have been learned from the British data collection experience. First, research has begun to show that the manner in which searches are conducted may greatly influence any resulting racial animosity surrounding police action. Research indicates that, although a search may be procedurally correct, when it is conducted confrontationally or in an uncivil or authoritarian manner, the result can be profoundly alienating.[117] Thus, the manner in which a search is conducted may be a major cause of particular complaints or dissatisfaction.

Second, some searches are conducted in response to specific incidents, information, and/or calls from the public. These are low-discretion searches. Other high-discretion searches are the result of proactive policing. Recognizing these differences may allow for a richer and more complete analysis of the data once they are collected.

Third, the initial research on data collection in Great Britain illustrates the complexities of measuring police disengagement. FitzGerald argues that a clear statistical relationship exists between the reduction in searches and the rise in crime in spring 1999. For example, searches produced 12 percent of all arrests in 1998, and by mid-1999, the number had fallen to under 9 percent of all arrests.[118] FitzGerald cautions that additional analyses are necessary to determine whether the reduction of searches had any direct influence on the rise in crime.[119] The possibility of police disengagement in Great Britain underscores the need for more systematic research on the relationship between data collection, search rates, and increases in crime to fully evaluate the successes or problems of initial stop-and-search data collection efforts.

Recommendations for Traffic-Stop Data Collection Systems

In implementing any data collection system, a primary consideration must be the feasibility of collecting the data. Police must collect sufficient data for meaningful analysis while creating a data collection system that is manageable and causes minimal inconvenience to citizens, officers, and other police administrators. For these reasons, each locality or jurisdiction may decide to balance considerations of time, officer safety, and convenience differently. This chapter offers recommendations for collecting data on traffic-stops and searches.[120] The recommendations are limited to traffic-stops for two reasons: all of the selected sites included in this analysis, with the exception of London, limited their data collection to traffic-stops; and jurisdictions that develop a successful traffic-stop protocol can then adjust their data collection mechanisms to meet the different needs of pedestrian-stop data collection.

For the purposes of this guide, a "stop" is defined as any time an officer initiates contact with a vehicle resulting in the detention of an individual and/or vehicle. Although jurisdictions may decide to widen or limit the scope of their data collection process, at a minimum data should be collected on all stops regardless of whether a warning or citation is issued. Much of the anecdotal evidence about racial profiling involves motorists who allege they were stopped for "driving the wrong car," "driving in the wrong place," or minor equipment violations. In many cases, these individuals were never issued a written warning or citation. Such incidents will only be captured in a data collection system that monitors all traffic-stops, regardless of outcome. Only by documenting all stops can a law enforcement organization gain information about the nature and scope of the alleged problem.

Local Task Force

Local jurisdictions will differ on the type of data that they will want to collect and the methodologies they will employ to collect information. However, a critical first step to any data collection design process is to convene a task force composed of representatives from law enforcement, members of the community, and citizen group representatives. Although this guide provides recommendations and models for data collection, a local task force is best able to recognize the specific needs of community members and police within a particular jurisdiction.

Additionally, we recommend that local jurisdictions develop a relationship with an academic or research partner. During the data collection design phase, local jurisdictions should consider who is going to analyze the stop-and-search data. When possible, the local jurisdiction should include members of the analysis team as part of the data collection design process. Knowing how the analysis will be conducted and what is needed for analysis is a critical step in the data collection design process.

Data Collection Pilot Program

In addition to gaining valuable guidance from a local task force, individual jurisdictions should allow 3 to 6 months as a test period for any data collection program. A pilot phase for data collection allows local jurisdictions to modify data collection elements, methodologies, and auditing procedures as needs arise.

If the first round of analysis determines that new elements need to be collected or changes need to be made to the data collection procedure, the data collection system should be flexible enough to allow for changes with minimal inconvenience and expense.

Data Collection Design

Any opportunity to streamline data collection efforts should be seized, and at least two opportunities exist. First, for those jurisdictions that have laptop computers or MDTs capable of running software, the easiest way to collect the data will be to use pulldown menus for each data collection category. For those jurisdictions that do not have such capabilities, San Jose's simple alpha code system enables the relevant data to be captured easily and quickly via the dispatcher or an MDT unit that cannot run windows. In San Jose, officers carry a pocket-sized laminated, color-coded card that assists them in recording the appropriate alpha codes for each designated category.

Additionally, we recommend that jurisdictions use existing data collection systems (dispatch information, citations, officer logs) to minimize the burden of additional data collection efforts. By linking current data collection processes with new study-specific information, local jurisdictions can minimize both cost and officer inconvenience.

Data Collection Elements

To discuss which data should be collected by local jurisdictions, we have categorized elements into two parts. The first set of elements in any traffic-stop study should be data that are routinely collected during normal traffic-stop operations. The second set of elements is to be collected specifically to assess questions of racial profiling in stop-and-search practices.

We recommend that jurisdictions assign a stop identification code to each dispatch or MDT communication for traffic-stops. The stop identification code should correspond to a unique identification number on new stop-and-search data collection forms or computer entries. This process allows jurisdictions to link information that they routinely collect on traffic-stops with additional information (either forms or computerized entries) specifically recommended for stop-and-search data collection. For example, if an officer normally calls in the license number and description of the vehicle stopped, the location of the stop, and his or her badge number, the officer would simply add a number identifying the data collection sheet or computerized entry to this dispatch. To further reduce officer workload, the unique identification numbers could also be attached to citations, search/inventory forms, or other routinely collected sources of information to be automatically linked with study-specific data elements.

The unique identification number can be used at a later date to match dispatch and study-specific information. During the analysis phase of their study, jurisdictions may determine which information from the dispatch records will be matched with stop-and-search study-specific records. The elements recommended for collecting routine dispatch or traffic-stop operations are described in the following section.

Routine Data Collection Elements

Date, time, and location of the stop. Collecting these items is essential for analyzing traffic-stop data. The data assist law enforcement by providing a context for stops made by enabling staff to determine where and when stops are occurring. This information could include the police precinct, the street address or intersection, and mile marker or exit. Some of the officers who have reacted negatively to the collection of stop-and-search data have raised an important issue. To fully understand why an officer chooses to stop a particular vehicle one must know the context of the situation. Was the stop part of a particular operation? Was the officer in a neighborhood of predominantly one race or ethnicity? By collecting basic information on the date and location of the stop, a department can begin to measure it in context. Additionally, the date, time, and location of the stop are critical components of future audits of traffic-stop data.

License number, state, and description of vehicle stopped. To ensure the accuracy of data collection procedures, a systematic mechanism for cross-checking data should be implemented. By recording the car's license number and state in which it is registered, staff can cross-check the data entered with department of motor vehicle (DMV) information.

In addition, many officers report that the decision to stop a vehicle may sometimes be due to the type of vehicle (e.g., rental) or a combination of the type of vehicle and the characteristics of its driver. Collecting this information allows departments to understand how often this type of stop occurs.

Length of stop. Anecdotal evidence includes incidents involving stops for extended periods. To discern whether this is a problem in a particular jurisdiction, officers should, with the assistance of the dispatcher, record the time at which a stop commenced and at which it ended.

Name and identification number of the officers who initiated or participated in the stop. One of the most controversial aspects of stop-and-search data collection is whether to collect the identity of the officer making the stop. There are several analytical advantages to recording these data. Adopting such an approach enables organizations to identify potential problem officers who may be disproportionately stopping minorities. In this sense, the data collection process functions as an early warning system, alerting management to problems and allowing them to investigate possible extenuating circumstances and, if necessary, to intervene early with counseling, training, or some other intervention.

Within this selected site analysis, San Jose, San Diego, and North Carolina do not collect the identity of the officers involved in a stop. By contrast, in New Jersey and Great Britain, the name and identity of the officer is included in the data collection process. Research from the few sites suggests that collection of officer identification can engender considerable officer and/or union opposition and disengagement.

An alternative to officer identification may be the use of unit or district information. This option provides a way to analyze the data within a meaningful unit of analysis (section/specific force) but allows agencies to collect data without requiring the identity of the officer. The purpose of recording the identity of the officer should be to diagnose and remedy problems as part of an early warning system. As New Jersey Attorney General Farmer stated: "It [data collection] is definitely supposed to be part of an early warning system that enables us to identify a potential problem, go in and fix it rather than waiting for it to fester. For it to be an early warning system, we didn't see any way to do it unless we had officer identification."

Departments should consider a procedure that requires the officer's identity to be recorded but uses the data primarily for training and support. Officers identified as engaging in any unusual pattern of vehicle stops would review the information with their immediate supervisors. If this pattern (or a similarly unusual pattern) persists, the behavior would be brought to the attention of the human resources unit of the department, and assistance/training would be offered to the officer. If these two steps are followed and the officer still behaves in a disturbing manner in traffic-stops, the matter should be dealt with using the department's normal disciplinary procedures.

Study-Specific Data Collection Elements

It is recommended that this second set of data be collected on all traffic-stops, regardless of whether a citation, search, or arrest is made. These elements could also be linked to existing forms or data entry.

Date of birth. Some jurisdictions collect age in two general categories, juvenile or adult, but it is recommended that officers record the exact age of the individual being stopped. This can be accomplished by having the officer record the date of birth that appears on the driver's license.

The reason for collecting exact age is two general categories such as juvenile or adult may conceal age distinctions. For example, the preliminary analysis of San Jose's data indicates that 97 percent of persons stopped were labeled adults, compared to 3 percent who were classified as minors. This finding indicates a need for more precise measurement. Additionally, national survey data indicate that young Black Americans disproportionally report the perception of being stopped by the police because of both their race and their age.[121] To address these concerns, data on the age of the person stopped should be available for analysis.

Gender. Many departments already collect information on the gender of persons stopped. This practice was established in some departments after the filing of several lawsuits alleging sexual harassment by male officers toward female motorists they stopped. Information about the gender of individuals stopped is important in stop-and-search data collection systems. Analysis of national survey data indicates that Black males perceive that they are being stopped more often than Black females or Whites of either sex.[122] Thus, the ability to disaggregate gender can be an important analytical tool.

Race or ethnicity. Unlike age and gender, which appear on an individual's driver's license, discerning race or ethnicity requires either a verbal inquiry of the individual or an officer's subjective determination. Since a verbal inquiry risks exacerbating tensions during a potentially tense encounter, to minimize inconvenience and maximize officer safety, we recommend using the officer's perception of race or ethnicity. Since an officer's perception of race or ethnicity gives rise to the problem of racial profiling, the officer's perception is an appropriate means of ascertaining race or ethnicity. Whether the officer correctly ascertains the race or ethnicity of the driver is less important than being able to analyze whether, having perceived the driver is a person of color, the officer treats the person fairly.

For data collection purposes, we recommend the following racial and ethnic categories:

❑ White.
❑ Black.
❑ Asian, Pacific Islander.
❑ Native American.
❑ Middle Eastern, East Indian.
❑ Hispanic.

Local jurisdictions may choose to alter these racial categories to more appropriately reflect the racial and ethnic demographics of their population. To assist the officer in assessing the ethnicity of an individual, it is suggested that the officer assess and record any racial identification information after using both of the following subjective tools: visual and verbal contact with the individual and the surname of the individual. Additionally, jurisdictions may want to consider whether an officer should be able to check two racial categories when the individual appears to be of mixed racial origin. While intending to more accurately reflect the ethnic diversity of a community, we believe that detailed ethnic breakdowns inevitably miss some groups and do an injustice to the rich ethnic heritage of most Americans.

Reason for the stop. The reason an officer gives for stopping a vehicle is one of the most important pieces of information that will be collected. Although there are many reasons why an individual might be stopped, a key design issue is not only to simplify this category sufficiently to allow manageable collection but also to provide for measurement precise enough to accurately monitor discretion. Discretion is at the core of a law enforcement officer's job, and it permits innovative, flexible problem solving. However, it also provides opportunities for conscious and subconscious racial discrimination to affect decisionmaking. The level of discretion involved in traffic-stops varies considerably. At times, officers respond to externally generated information. For example, when a person places a 911 call providing a description of a crime, officers have little discretion but to respond. This type of low-discretion situation might be analyzed differently from other law enforcement actions because it is based on an external source rather than an individual officer's discretionary determination. Similarly, if an officer observes a driver failing to stop at a red light or driving 30 miles above the speed limit, the officer may feel obliged to pull over the driver. This type of officer-initiated low-discretion situation differs dramatically from an officer-initiated high-discretion stop such as when an officer stops a vehicle with underinflated tires, a soiled license plate, or traveling 4 miles above the speed limit. In both the low-discretion and the high-discretion stops, the driver has violated the law, but officers vary more often in their responses to high-discretion situations.

Disparate treatment is more likely to occur in high-discretion than low-discretion circumstances. Consequently, the data collection systems should be designed so that analysts can disaggregate the level of discretion available to the officer at the time of the stop and whether the stop was based on external information such as an all-points bulletin or a 911 call.

Although jurisdictions and/or localities may collect different elements that correspond appropriately with local enforcement patterns, we recommend the categories listed in table 2. Departments should review stop and citation practices within their own jurisdiction to determine appropriate reasons for stopping motorists.

Unfortunately, the reason for the stop category is often oversimplified. San Jose's preliminary analysis demonstrates the problems of narrowly defining this category. San Jose designated only four reasons that a vehicle was stopped: vehicle code violation, penal code violation, municipal code violation, and a stop based on an all-points or be-on-the-lookout notice. Its first analysis revealed that 99 percent of the time the reason for the stop was a vehicle code violation, a broad category that fails to distinguish among moving violations, nonmoving violations, equipment violations, and hazardous moving violations. This type of broad categorization obfuscates distinctions among the various types of violations and indicates the need for a more precise measurement.

Disposition or outcome of the stop. The disposition of each traffic-stop should be collected. While there are many police disposition codes relevant to traffic-stops, departments should use a system that limits the

Table 2	Reasons for Stopping Motorists

Reason for Stop	Examples
Hazardous moving violation	Stoplight or stop sign violation, driving 10 miles or more above the speed limit
Nonhazardous moving violation	Failure to signal when changing lanes, driving less than 10 miles above the speed limit
Externally generated information stop	911 call or all-points bulletin
Vehicle equipment violations/defects	Broken headlight or brake light, underinflated tires, etc.
Investigatory stop	Belief of criminal activity based on observation
Seat belt violation	
Driving while impaired	
Courtesy stop/citizen assistance	
Other motor vehicle violation	

complexity and volume of codes to be collected. Officers should be allowed to designate more than one disposition code, if necessary. The following disposition codes are recommended:

- ❑ Oral warning.
- ❑ Written warning (where used).
- ❑ Arrest made.
- ❑ Arrest by warrant.
- ❑ Criminal citation.
- ❑ Traffic citation—hazardous.
- ❑ Traffic citation—nonhazardous.
- ❑ Courtesy service/citizen assist.
- ❑ No action taken.

Whether a search was conducted. This is a complex but valuable item to collect. While there are sundry legal and operational factors involved in collecting information about searches, such information should be collected. For most officers, searching is a relatively rare activity; so, ordinarily, most officers will not be completing the series of inquiries that follow. Still, the following information should be collected:

- ❑ Was a search conducted (yes/no)?
- ❑ What type of search was conducted?
    - ■ Vehicle
    - ■ Driver
    - ■ Passenger or passengers
- ❑ What was the basis for the search?
    - ■ Visible contraband
    - ■ Odor of contraband
    - ■ Canine alert
    - ■ Inventory search prior to impoundment
    - ■ Consent search
- ❑ Was contraband found (yes/no)?
- ❑ Was property seized (yes/no)?
- ❑ Describe the nature and quantity of the contraband seized or found.[123]
- ❑ Comment Box that allows officers to put in any contextual information that appears relevant to the search, such as a strategic initiative.

For some of the above categories, an officer can check more than one category. When using a computerized data collection system, the categories can be defaulted to "no" to speed data collection in cases where a search was not conducted.

Although it may seem easier to omit search information from the process, it serves two valuable functions. First, search information provides local jurisdictions with a sense of the quantity and quality of searches being conducted, the characteristics of those searches, and their productivity. Productivity refers to the number of searches that result in arrests or seizures, the nature of those arrests, and the quality of the seizures. Such information allows local jurisdictions to appropriately allocate resources to productive search techniques. Second, information about searches allows departments to assess whether certain groups are disproportionally targeted for searches.

Mechanisms for Ensuring Data Integrity

To ensure the accuracy of data collection processes, departments should implement a mechanism for spot-checking or cross-checking the data. Several possibilities exist. Nearly all traffic-stops conducted by officers in the United States involve an officer transmitting to the dispatcher that a stop is being made. This is normal police procedure in most communities. It increases officer safety by notifying the dispatcher that the officer is leaving the police vehicle to talk to a citizen. It also informs the dispatcher that the officer is involved with an action and may not be available to take another call. These stops are part of the CAD file in most agencies and could be reviewed to ensure that all stops result in a traffic-stop data form being completed.

Using the license plate number and the state the vehicle is registered in, staff can spot-check reports by cross-checking data collected with the relevant state DMV information. Some DMVs have on file the race of the licensee or a photograph of the license holder. This information could be used on a limited basis to verify the race and ethnicity information on the completed data collection forms.

An additional auditing mechanism involves ongoing customer satisfaction surveys that many departments use. Most of these surveys randomly poll those who have called the police for assistance. The respondents are asked a few questions about the quality of the service they received and their satisfaction with it. This approach could be useful in traffic-stops. During this survey, information could be acquired about the race of the person stopped and the reason for the stop. This information could be used to verify the information collected by the officer.

Such a survey helps to ensure the accuracy of data and provides management with useful information about the quality of stops and searches from the perspective of the individual stopped. As in earlier instances, the information should be used principally for training purposes and not for officer discipline.

Data Analysis and Future Research

The limited studies available concerning disparate stop-and-search patterns during traffic-stops raise complex analytical issues. Local jurisdictions must coordinate data collection design efforts with a designated data collection team. Where possible, local jurisdictions should partner with statisticians at local universities, colleges, or junior colleges or work with members of internal research units.

The three most vexing problems involve assessing why an individual officer decides to stop a particular vehicle, measuring the populations that put themselves at risk of being stopped by their actions or the actions of others (a base violation rate), and comparing pedestrian stops to appropriate street populations (or street violator populations).

Assessing Police Discretion

Many officers have spoken of the difficulty in quantifying the decision to stop. They have noted that the decision to stop a vehicle is the result of several factors including the behavior of the operator of the vehicle, the officer's experience, the departmental policies and procedures, the crime problems faced by a particular neighborhood, and specific police tactics. Although no quantitative survey can accurately measure all the factors involved in an officer's decision, the collection of data can provide some aggregate estimates about the behavior of officers as well as the criminal behavior of certain population groups.

By collecting information about a phenomenon that is almost invisible to review at the moment, a law enforcement agency can identify a typical pattern of behavior of its officers and discern if outliers exist. This analysis could be done for individual officers or for individual neighborhoods. Data collection could determine, for example, that a typical officer stops 10 cars per shift and issues 4 citations. Once this information is known, the behavior of all officers can be evaluated by this measure. If an officer is stopping 50 cars in a shift, that officer may be working very hard in an area or may be causing increased community resentment in a particular neighborhood. Similarly, if the officer who stops 50 motorists only issues 4 citations, this may identify a training issue regarding why the hit rate of this officer is so much lower than others. There may be legitimate reasons for this kind of variation, but currently, most police departments do not even know whether this kind of variability exists.

The collection of this kind of information enables an agency to track changes over time. If departments were regularly collecting information on the characteristics of traffic-stops, they would be able to detect trends in the use of this law enforcement tactic. If the number of stops decreased drastically in one section of a community, the data would alert officials to this change. Similarly, if one area is marked by an increase in stops of Asian motorists, a department could investigate to determine the cause of this increase. In addition, having the data would allow departments to respond more quickly to complaints from community groups of racial profiling.

Constructing a Comparative Benchmark

Once a law enforcement agency begins to gather traffic-stop data, what steps should be undertaken to understand and interpret the data? One important step is to bring the agency, community members, and other interested persons together to construct a comparative benchmark to determine whether minority individuals are being stopped disproportionately. This benchmark is also important for determining whether poststop law enforcement actions are being directed at minorities in a disproportionate manner. If a substantial disparity is found, is there a nondiscriminatory explanation or justification for the disparity?

By themselves, the characteristics of traffic-stops are difficult to interpret. For example, if, after collecting data, a particular city discovers that 65 percent of its traffic-stops on a particular highway are of Hispanic drivers, that percentage by itself does not reveal much. The city must compare that percentage to an appropriate benchmark, which ideally could be the proportion of Hispanic traffic violators on the highways where the stops occurred. Thus, the 65 percent stopping rate would be proportionate if 65 percent of the violators on this highway were Hispanic but would be disproportionate if only 20 percent of the violators were Hispanic. The city could determine whether the disparity correlates with a disproportionate allocation of police resources to minority residential areas and, if it does so, whether this correlation explains the disparity.

Generally, there are two different types of comparative benchmarks: those that are external to the traffic-stop data and those that may be generated from within the data set. These benchmarks can be used in conjunction or separately.

External benchmarks involve developing an estimate of the percentages of persons who are at risk for being stopped on roads that are patrolled by the law enforcement agency by racial or ethnic group. These benchmarks may be used to measure persons who are violating traffic laws on particular roadways or, alternatively, may simply travel on these roads. In analyzing police activity on a particular highway or road, the stationary and rolling surveys planned by Zingraff and conducted by Lamberth provide ways to calculate a violator rate broken down by race. However, it may be appropriate to construct benchmarks that simply measure the racial percentages of vehicle drivers on particular roadways.

Some jurisdictions have sought to use residential population data, broken down by race, to estimate the racial percentages of persons using the jurisdiction's roads. This breakdown may be useful, if done properly. First, it is important to ensure that the population data are sufficiently current. The 2000 census would be a more appropriate description of population demographics than older census estimates. Second, because the age demographics for different racial groups may vary, it is vital that the residential benchmark be applied only to individuals who are of legal driving age. Other available data concerning a person's access to vehicles reported by race may help jurisdictions refine the residential population benchmark. Third, residential population benchmarks are least appropriate for examining the racial demographics of individuals stopped by the police who reside outside that particular jurisdiction.

Various internal benchmarks may be developed. For example, a jurisdiction could compare traffic-stop data of the same unit (or the same officer) over time or could compare that data for several units (or several individual officers) that patrol the same or similar areas. Additionally, data on speeding tickets and searches may be analyzed to determine if minority drivers are disproportionately ticketed or searched. Finally, data on searches may be analyzed to compare the percentages of persons searched, by race, with the corresponding hit rates (searches producing contraband) for different racial groups.

More research is needed to determine the most useful way to analyze data on stops and searches. By experimenting with various benchmark comparisons, practical methods can be designed.

Conclusion and Recommendations

The challenge that confronts American police organizations is how to sustain the historic decline in rates of criminal activity while enhancing police legitimacy in the eyes of the communities they serve. Appropriately addressing allegations of racial profiling is central to this new mission. Historically, police have defined their purpose as regulatory—ensuring the greatest possible order. Their task was reactive and involved responding to obvious signs of disorder, such as emergency calls. Realizing the profound limitations of this model, the community policing strategy began to use information, technology, research, and data to engage officers in more effective and better managed policing by anticipating and disrupting the causes of disorder. Nationwide, police departments have begun using information and technology to measure and identify crime clusters and develop strategies to intervene and disrupt violent crime before it occurs.

Local and state jurisdictions that have begun to collect data point to a number of benefits of a well-planned traffic-stop data collection system. Some of these advantages include the following:

❑ Police forces committed to improving legitimacy find that measurement of police activity is a critical first step toward effective management.

❑ Data collection sends a clear message that racial profiling is inconsistent with effective policing and equal protection.

❑ Having available data moves the conversation within the community away from rhetoric and accusations to a discussion about the effective deployment of police resources.

❑ In contrast to a rigid set of guidelines, the data collection approach allows a fluid and local determination of how to deploy law enforcement resources.

❑ The process of collecting data begins to change behavior of line officers and supervisors.

As state and local law enforcement agencies develop data collection designs to address community concerns about racial profiling in police stops and searches, DOJ can play an increasingly important role. By providing information and technical assistance to state and local law enforcement agencies, DOJ can encourage localities to adopt suitable racial profiling data collection systems. To facilitate this goal, the authors recommend that DOJ should:

❑ Sponsor a Web site for disseminating up-to-date information about racial profiling data collection system designs, providing sample data collection forms, and allowing a forum for discussion of common obstacles.

❑ Encourage and fund demonstration projects for determining best practices for data collection and analysis. At the time this guide was drafted, only a few jurisdictions had developed and implemented comprehensive data collection systems. Since then, and as this guide goes to press, numerous law enforcement jurisdictions have started collecting data. In the light of this increased data collection activity, and as a followup to this guide, DOJ should fund a Best Practices Guide to examine and evaluate emerging traffic-stop policies, data collection strategies, training, and analysis techniques.

❑ Assist jurisdictions in designing statistical benchmarks and determining comparative populations. Such projects might include an academic workshop on the ways to construct a statistical benchmark and meaningfully analyze traffic-stop data.

❑ Recognize and reward pioneering efforts in racial profiling data collection, and provide encouragement for other jurisdictions to follow their lead.

❑ Create requirements in federal funding to ensure design and implementation of state and local traffic-stop data collection protocols.

❑ Develop federal funding programs for software, technical assistance, and data analysis grants for state and local agencies.

❑ Foster partnerships between DOJ and the U.S. Attorney's Offices that would encourage U.S. Attorneys to meet with their local community policing partners to discuss the prospect of voluntary data collection efforts. To further this goal, DOJ could host an information session on current data collection efforts and strategies.

❑ Develop a traffic-stop training curriculum that specifically address the issues of racial profiling for use by state and local departments.

Contact Information

Authors

Professor Deborah A. Ramirez
Northeastern University School of Law
400 Huntington Avenue
Boston, MA 02115
617–373–4629
Fax: 617–373–5056
E-mail: d.ramirez@nunet.neu.edu

Professor Jack McDevitt
Director, Center for Criminal Justice
    Policy Research
400 Churchill Hall
Northeastern University
Boston, MA 02115
E-mail: ja.mcdevitt@nunet.neu.edu

Amy Farrell
Doctoral Candidate
Law, Policy and Society Program
400 Churchill Hall
Northeastern University
Boston, MA 02115
E-mail: afarrell@lynx.neu.edu

Site Data Collection Contacts

San Jose
Captain Rob Davis
Bureau of Technical Assistance
855 North San Pedro Street
San Jose, CA 95110
408–277–5716

San Diego
Tony McElroy
Special Assistant to the Chief
1401 Broadway
San Diego, CA 92101–5729

North Carolina
Lt. Col. W.M. Autry
Department of Crime Control and
    Public Safety
North Carolina Highway Patrol
512 North Salisbury Street
Raleigh, NC 27626–0590

New Jersey
Attorney General John Farmer
State of New Jersey
P.O. Box 080
Trenton, NJ 08625

Great Britain
New Scotland Yard
Broadway
London, England
SW1H OBG

Notes

1. *Attorney General's Conference on Strengthening Police-Community Relationships, Report on the Proceedings,* Washington, DC: U.S. Department of Justice, June 9–10, 1999, at 22–23.

2. The U.S. Supreme Court has addressed the issue of ethnicity and immigration stops in *United States* v. *Brignoni-Ponce* 422 U.S. 873 (1975) and *United States* v. *Martinez-Fuerte* 428 U.S. 543 (1976). More recently, the Ninth Circuit addressed the use of race in border stops in *United States* v. *Montero-Camargo*, 208 F. 3d 1122 (9th Cir. 2000).

3. Gallup Poll Organization Poll Release, *Racial Profiling Is Seen as Widespread, Particularly Among Young Black Men,* Princeton, NJ: Gallup Poll Organization, December 9, 1999, at 1.

4. Gallup Poll Organization Poll Release, see note 3, at 1.

5. Bureau of Justice Statistics, *Criminal Victimization and Perceptions of Community Safety in 12 Cities, 1998,* Washington, DC: U.S. Department of Justice, May 1999 (NCJ 173940).

6. David Harris, *Driving While Black: Racial Profiling on Our Nation's Highways,* Washington, DC: American Civil Liberties Union, 1999.

7. Mark Hosenball, "It Is Not the Act of a Few Bad Apples: Lawsuit Shines the Spotlight on Allegations of Racial Profiling by New Jersey State Troopers," *Newsweek,* May 17, 1999, at 34–35.

8. Richard Weizel, "Lawmaker Pushes for Racial Profiling Bill," *Boston Globe,* May 2, 1999, at D21.

9. *Wilkins* v. *Maryland State Police,* Civil Action No. CCB–93–483, Maryland Federal District Court (1993). For a discussion of the settlement, see John Lamberth, "Driving While Black: A Statistician Proves That Prejudice Still Rules the Road," *Washington Post,* August 16, 1999, at C1.

10. Lamberth, see note 9. For a discussion of the Lamberth study, see David Harris, "The Stories, the Statistics, and the Law: Why Driving While Black Matters," *Minnesota Law Review* 84(2), 1999, at 280–281.

11. Lamberth, see note 9, at 4.

12. *State of New Jersey* v. *Pedro Soto et al.,* Superior Court of New Jersey, 734 A.2d 350, 1996.

13. The stop and arrest information was compiled using patrol charts, radio logs, and traffic tickets for selected dates from April 1988 to May 1991.

14. Peter Verniero and Paul Zoubek, *New Jersey Attorney General's Interim Report of the State Police Review Team Regarding Allegations of Racial Profiling (N.J. Interim Rep.)*, April 20, 1999.

15. Verniero and Zoubek, see note 14, at 27–28.

16. Kevin Flynn, "State Cites Racial Inequality in New York Police Searches," *New York Times*, December 1, 1999, at 22.

17. New York Attorney General, New York City Police *"Stop and Frisk" Practices: A Report to the People of New York From the Office of the Attorney General*, New York, NY: December 1, 1999, at 95.

18. *Statistics on Race and the Criminal Justice System: A Home Office Publication Under Section 95 of the Criminal Justice Act of 1991*, London, England: Home Office, 1998, chapters 3 and 4.

19. *The UK in Figures*, London, England: Office of National Statistics, Government Statistical Service, 1999.

20. Marian FitzGerald, *Searches in London, Interim Evaluation of Year One of the Programme of Action*, London, England: Home Office, August 1999, at 21.

21. For a discussion of this practice, see Gary Webb, "Driving While Black," *Esquire Magazine*, April 1999, at 119–127.

22. New York Attorney General, see note 17, at 141–145.

23. Marion FitzGerald, *Final Report Into Stop-and-Search*, London, England: Metropolitan Police, 1999.

24. This idea has been perpetuated by some police training materials. For example, in the mid-1980s, the Florida Department of Highway Safety and Motor Vehicles issued guidelines for the police on common characteristics of drug couriers that warned officers to be suspicious of drivers who do not "fit the vehicle" and "ethnic groups associated with the drug trade." For a discussion of this practice, see O.W. Wisotsky, *Beyond the War on Drugs: Overcoming a Failed Public Policy*, Buffalo, NY: Prometheus Books, 1990.

25. Note that only a limited number of empirical studies have examined the relationship between an individual's race and the probability that they are carrying contraband. More research is needed to address such questions.

26. Lamberth, see note 9.

27. Verniero and Zaubek, see note 14. Note that the New Jersey report is based on a sample size of only 78 searches. Although the hit rate of 38 percent for Latinos was higher than for Whites or Blacks, the smaller number of searches involving Latinos makes any conclusion about the proportionality of those searches more difficult to determine statistically.

28. New York Attorney General, see note 17, at 111.

29. U.S. Customs Service, *Personal Searches of Air Passengers Results: Positive and Negative*, Washington, DC, 1998, at 1. For a discussion of the Customs study, see Harris, note 10, at 277–288.

30. FitzGerald, see note 23.

31. National research conducted by the Substance Abuse and Mental Health Services Administration (SAMHSA) *National Household Survey of Drug Abuse* indicates that the rate at which Blacks use illegal drugs is 8.2 percent, only slightly higher than the White or Hispanic rates, both at 6.1 percent. This research indicates that the vast majority of people across all racial groups do not use drugs and should not be seen as targets of suspicion. Similarly, the National Institute of Drug Abuse found that 12 percent to 14 percent of those who abuse drugs are Black. This percentage mirrors the proportion of Blacks in the general population. For more information, see National Clearinghouse for Alcohol and Drug Information, Research and Statistics, *National Household Survey on Drug Abuse*, Washington, DC: U.S. Department of Health and Human Services, 1998, at 16.

32. The racial demographics of arrest statistics for narcotics show more Blacks, Hispanics, and minorities tend to be arrested on drug charges than Whites. However, most drug possession and distribution go undetected. Those activities are private and conducted outside the ambit of police view. Only a small percentage of these crimes are given the attention of law enforcement. Thus, the number of drug arrests may only reflect law enforcement patterns.

33. Just as we do not allow insurance companies to charge differential life insurance rates to women because they live longer than men, we ought not allow empirical racial profiling to impose costs on the entire community of color. It would be unfair to stigmatize an entire community based on the conduct of a few. By allowing police to use race as a factor in determining whom to stop-and-search, many innocent Black and Hispanic individuals are subjected to searches. For more discussion on this issue, see Randall Kennedy, *Race, Crime and the Law*, New York, NY: Pantheon Books, 1997, at 147.

34. San Jose Police Department, *Vehicle Stop Demographic Study: First Report*, San Jose, CA, December 1999.

35. Julie Lynem, "San Jose Police Study: Race in Arrest Patterns," *San Francisco Chronicle*, March 25, 1999, at A17.

36. Joe Rodriques, "No Refuge From Racism Behind the Wheel," *San Jose Mercury News*, March 29, 1999, at 1B.

37. Julie Ha, "Groups Seek Data on Race-Based Police Stops," *Los Angeles Times*, April 16, 1999, at B3.

38. Ha, see note 37, at B3.

39. SJPD's prior protocol already required officers to indicate whether the stop was being made on a male or female. Under that protocol, an officer used a code to indicate whether the driver was a female (11–95X) or male (11–95).

40. In San Jose, a municipal code violation refers to laws that forbid activities such as cruising or continuing to drive in circles on a main road.

41. This code is used when no enforcement action is taken, such as when an officer stops a driver for a moving or equipment violation and issues a verbal warning instead of a citation.

42. Lynem, see note 35.

43. However, San Jose's initial analysis of its data collection indicates that many calls were cleared with incomplete information, sometimes due to special enforcement activities such as radar patrols.

44. After preliminary analysis of the first 3 months of data, San Jose determined that they would need to refine the traffic-stop categories because nearly all calls fell into the vehicle code violation category, making any analysis of the reason for the stop less meaningful.

45. Including the type of contraband seized and a description of it should not be difficult. Once contraband is seized, police must record such information in their routine police reports.

46. Of course, even though the data are not tabulated by officer identification number, since the name of the officer, the time, date of the stop, and the computer on which the data were recorded are potentially available, the identification of the officer is not truly anonymous. It could be obtained, but it is not routinely collected and analyzed.

47. Although the study began on June 1, 1999, the Crime Analysis Unit decided to conduct its first report for stops generated from July 1 to September 30. This time period allowed SJPD to look at corresponding quarterly reports so that the data collection could be correlated with existing crime statistics.

48. Local news reports and editorials suggest that 1990 census estimates incorrectly represent the minority populations in California. See "Are Our Cops Colorblind," *San Jose Mercury News,* December 23, 1999; "Blacks and Latinos Stopped More: San Jose Police Release Traffic-Stop Report," *San Jose Mercury News,* December 18, 1999.

49. This was done by using 1990 census data and 1995 California Department of Finance data estimates on population increases in the state. SJPD then applied the same data population projections for the 1990–95 period to the 1995–99 period.

50. Note that the vast majority of citations during the study period were for speeding, not for equipment failure or vehicle code violations.

51. Some law enforcement organizations have put video cameras in patrol cars. They are usually located inside the car near the rearview mirror. Tapes are then stored for a certain period. Supervisors review some tapes and use them for training purposes.

52. San Diego Police Department, Budget and Personnel, 1999.

53. San Diego Police Department, Historical Crime Rates, 1950–1999.

54. George Will, "Takes More Than Good Policing To Cut Crime," *Houston Chronicle,* August 23, 1999, at A18.

55. David Bejarano, *Racial Profiling: The San Diego Police Department's Response,* Internal Memo, Chief of Police, San Diego Police Department, November 9, 1999.

56. Michael Stetz and Kelly Thorton, "Cops To Collect Traffic Stop Racial Data," *San Diego Union Tribune,* February 5, 1999, at A1.

57. Stetz and Thorton, see note 56.

58. Doc Anthony Anderson, "They're Guilty of Driving—While Being Black or Brown," *San Diego Union Tribune,* December 24, 1998, at B9; Michael Stetz, "Stopped for Driving While Black: People of Color Commonly Are Pulled Over by Police for Little Apparent Reason," *San Diego Union Tribune,* December 13, 1999, at A1.

59. Stetz and Thorton, see note 56.

60. At the time of the drafting for this guide, San Diego officers were using paper forms to collect data because laptops had not yet been installed in patrol cars.

61. Stetz and Thorton, see note 56.

62. Interview with former San Diego Police Chief Jerry Sanders, March 1, 2000.

63. Stetz and Thorton, see note 56.

64. North Carolina Office of State Planning, State Demographics, 1997.

65. Demographic information provided by NCHP.

66. Lynn Bonner, "Bill Probes Traffic Stops for Driving While Black," *Raleigh News and Observer*, February 18, 1999.

67. The drug interdiction team is a small and distinct unit of troops whose mission is to uncover drug traffickers on the state and interstate highways. For a description of racial disparities in drug charges by the interdiction team, see Joseph Neff and Pat Stith, "Highway Drug Unit Focuses on Blacks," *Raleigh News and Observer*, July 28, 1996, at A1.

68. Joseph Neff, "Who's Being Stopped?" *Raleigh News and Observer*, February 19, 1999, at A2.

69. Press Release, Office of North Carolina Governor Jim Hunt, April 22, 1999.

70. There are no racial or ethnic data on North Carolina driver's licenses, but there is backup information available from the state bureau of motor vehicles. They collect it by asking an optional question about race and ethnicity. If unanswered, bureau staff record what they perceive.

71. Interview with NCHP Colonel Richard Holden, September 27, 1999.

72. These figures do not include the costs of additional training associated with using the data collection system.

73. The only indication of the number of verbal warning stops is based on estimates by individual troopers.

74. Blacks in North Carolina represent approximately 22 percent of the state population, and 22.6 percent of the motorists stopped by NCHP in January 2000 were Black. In the same study, of those searched, 31 percent were Black, and of those arrested 27 percent were Black. For a description of the preliminary data report, see "Spotlight on Stops," *Raleigh News and Observer*, March 9, 2000, at A16; Craig Jarvis, "Traffic Stops Aren't Linked to Race, First Report Shows," *Raleigh News and Observer*, March 3, 2000, at A3.

75. Annual Demographic Profile for New Jersey, New Jersey Department of Labor and Management, March 1999.

76. Interview with New Jersey Attorney General John Farmer, April 4, 2000.

77. Ralph Seigel, "Racial Profiling Anatomy of a Scandal," *New Jersey Reporter*, 28, May 1999, at 17–29.

78. *New Jersey* v. *Soto*, 734 A.2d 350, Superior Court of New Jersey (1996).

79. *New Jersey* v. *Soto*, 734 A.2d 350, Superior Court of New Jersey (1996).

80. Details of events leading up to the shooting are unclear. Troopers report that the van backed away from the officers and veered into the patrol car before sideswiping a car in oncoming traffic and that they fired shots because they perceived that the van was trying to get away. The occupants of the van claim that the van shifted out of gear, and they only backed into traffic as a response to police drawing their weapons. For a description of the event, see John Kifner and David Herszenhorn, "Racial Profiling at Crux of Inquiry Into Shooting by Troopers," *New York Times*, May, 8, 1998, at B1.

81. Michael Raphel and Kathy Barrett Calter, "State Police Reveal 75% of Arrests Along Turnpike Were of Minorities," *Star-Ledger*, February 10, 1999, at News 01.

82. Michael Raphel and Joe Donahue, "Turnpike Arrests 73% Minority," *Star-Ledger*, April 8, 1999, at News 01.

83. Joe Donahue, "Trooper Boss: Race Plays Role in Drug Crimes," *Star-Ledger*, February 28, 1999, at News 01.

84. In New Jersey, the attorney general oversees the activities of the state police.

85. Joint Application for Entry of Consent Decree, *United States* v. *State of New Jersey*, Civil Action 99–5970 (MLC), December 20, 1999 (consent decree).

86. Consent Decree, *see* note 85, at 29–33.

87. Letter from Martin Cronin, assistant attorney general, director of State Police Affairs in New Jersey, June 13, 2000 (on file with author).

88. Joint Application for Entry of Consent Decree, see note 85, at section 110.

89. Joint Application for Entry of Consent Decree, see note 85.

90. Interview with John Farmer, see note 76.

91. The attorney general cited the Officer of the Year Award within the state police as an example of past departmental emphasis on arrests. Traditionally, the award went to the officer making the highest number of arrests rather than any qualitative measure of good behavior, acts of valor, or assisting motorists.

92. The "other" category includes Pakistani, Somalian, and Indian.

93. Marian FitzGerald and Rae Sibbitt, *Ethnic Monitoring in Police Forces: A Beginning*, London, England: Home Office, Research and Statistics Directorate, 1997, at 12.

94. Sir William MacPherson, *The Stephen Lawrence Inquiry*, London, England: The Stationary Office, 1999, at 1.

95. MacPherson, see note 94, at 2, 3.

96. MacPherson, see note 94, at 4.

97. MacPherson, see note 94, at 6.

98. MacPherson, see note 94, at 4.

99. MacPherson, see note 94, at 312.

100. MacPherson, see note 94, at 334.

101. The seven pilot sites are Brixton, Charing Cross, Hounslow, Kingston, Limehouse, Plumstead, and Tottenham.

102. Great Britain has collected data on searches from 1996 to 2000.

103. Police and Criminal Evidence Act of 1983. For a discussion of PACE and its implementation, see FitzGerald, note 23.

104. For example, in Hounslow, voluntary stops and traffic stops will be included, but "stop and talks," where police and people on the street stop to converse, will not be included. Hence, most officer-initiated contacts will be recorded. Hounslow is just one of seven pilot sites participating in experimental data collection strategies.

105. English law allows this in limited circumstances. For example, when there is a gang fight, such searches might be authorized within 1 square mile for a short period. Such an action must be ratified in 24 hours by a superintendent.

106. In Hounslow, these 17 self-identification codes are already being used. Note that the self-identification categories are not the same as the ones police use to describe persons searched.

107. FitzGerald, see note 23, at 29.

108. Marian FitzGerald, *Stop-and-Search Interim Report*, London, England: The Stationary Office, 1999, at 63.

109. FitzGerald, see note 23, at 29.

110. FitzGerald, see note 23, at 29.

111. FitzGerald, see note 23, at 24.

112. FitzGerald, see note 23, at Figure 3:5.

113. FitzGerald, see note 23, at Figure 3:5.

114. FitzGerald, see note 23, at 21.

115. FitzGerald, see note 23, at 49.

116. FitzGerald, see note 23, at 52.

117. FitzGerald, see note 23, at 54.

118. Presentation to MPS Lay Advisor's Group—Written Remarks, February 15, 2000 (on file with author).

119. Marion FitzGerald, *The Relationship Between Police Searches and Crime*, January 24, 2000 (on file with author).

120. The recommendations offered in this guide arise from research on the selected sites highlighted in Chapter 4. Additionally, Houston, Philadelphia, Richmond, and many other local jurisdictions have graciously volunteered information and samples of their data collection forms, which were useful in designing these recommendations.

121. Gallup Poll, December 9, 1999. Seventy-two percent of Black men between the ages of 18 and 34 report that they perceived they were stopped by the police because of their race.

122. Gallup Poll, see note 121. Only 40 percent of Black women between the ages of 18 and 34 reported a perception that they were stopped by the police because of their race compared to 72 percent of men of the same age category.

123. The question of nature and quantity of contraband could be categorized by local jurisdictions. Most officers will be unable to give exact quantities of drugs or other contraband, but it is important to distinguish small amounts of drugs, guns, or other contrabands from major quantities. As we saw in the example from the New Jersey attorney general, officers may be making many stops that result in small "finds" of drugs or guns, but such stops do not uncover higher quantities of contraband associated with trafficking. By having some qualitative information about the quantities seized in searches, departments can monitor the effectiveness of their traffic-stop efforts.